A FUTURE FOR EVERYONE

A FUTURE
FOR EVERYONE

Innovative Social Responsibility
and Community Partnerships

EDITED BY
DAVID MAURRASSE
WITH CYNTHIA JONES

Routledge
NEW YORK AND LONDON

Published in 2004 by
Routledge
29 West 35th Street
New York, New York 10001
www.routledge-ny.com

Published in Great Britain by
Routledge
11 New Fetter Lane
London EC4P 4EE
www.routledge.co.uk

10 9 8 7 6 5 4 3 2 1

Library of Congress Cataloging-in-Publication Data
A future for everyone : innovative social responsibility and community
partnerships / edited by David Maurrasse.
        p. cm.
Includes bibliographical references and index.
    ISBN 0-415-94452-X (hardcover : alk. paper) — ISBN 0-415-94453-8
(pbk. : alk. paper)
    1.   Social responsibility of business. 2. Community development. 3.
Digital divide. I. Marrausse, David, 1968-
✓ HD60.F87 2003
    658.4′08—dc22

Contents

ILLUSTRATIONS

Figures

Tables

Acknowledgments

This book is the result of a gigantic collective effort. Cynthia Jones was a major force in providing the glue and much of the work that led to the development of this effort. The concept for the book began with the idea for a conference on social responsibility held at Columbia University in 2001. Cynthia was also instrumental in making that "Symposium on Social Responsibility" a reality. The conference was sponsored by the initiative that I founded, the Center for Innovation in Social Responsibility (CISR), which would not exist without Manning Marable and the Institute for Research in African American Studies (IRAAS) at Columbia University, which provided CISR a home, seed funding, and financial management. Kecia Hayes, a former employee of IRAAS, also deserves specific thanks for all of her work in organizing the conference. The Annie E. Casey Foundation and the New York Community Trust (by way of Holly Delaney Cole) also provided important financial support that led to the creation of this book.

It was through a conversation with my editor, Ilene Kalish that the idea for the conference surfaced. I proposed this book as an idea, and she recommended that I organize a conference, which could lead to the creation of a manuscript. I dutifully followed that advice, and here we are. Ilene puts up with my constant flow of ideas and my very drafty drafts. It's a process!

Everyone involved in developing the original conference deserves thanks. Many of the presenters on that day, became the contributors in this book. Jonathan Cohen, Aida Rodriguez, Tyshammie Cooper, Carol Glazer, Perry Mehrling, Osagie Kingsley Obasogie, Frank Dixon, David N. Cox, and Heather Bent Tamir were all present on that October day and have stayed with this project up to this point. Allan J. Formicola was added as an author along the way. Gloria McKenna, Amy Hall, and Walid Michelin all presented on that day, and deserve recognition. Contributors to this book Sandra Harris, Joseph A. Pereira, Shana Brodnax, and Melissa Pearce. Together, we combined our pieces of the big picture, contributed to a unique dialogue, and created an interesting book. Thanks also go out to Jackie Bliss, who helped with editing. And, thanks to my mother, whose constant concern for people other than herself deeply informs my work.

Introduction

DAVID MAURRASSE

How do we create a future for everyone in a world where all people have a stake in society and an opportunity to succeed, even thrive? This book is about finding ways to create such opportunities. More specifically, I want to think about the roles that government, corporations, institutions, and nonprofit organizations can, should, and are playing in the creation of a common good. I'm especially interested in discussing how these players can come together to form effective partnerships in their local communities.

In the past, the role of trying to help society has been seen as the role of government agencies and volunteers. But, increasingly, nonprofit organizations, corporations, and institutions are now playing a more active role in the betterment of society. The venture of large institutions into this territory has raised some eyebrows. Some technology companies are emphasizing the need to bridge the "digital divide,"[1] and corporations of many types are prioritizing good neighborly behavior and partnerships with nonprofit organizations.[2] Shareholders have begun to influence significantly corporate behavior through, what has become known as, "socially responsible investing."[3] Universities want to be known as good "community partners,"[4] and many of the wealthy wish to be "strategic philanthropists." Corporate social responsibility, in itself, has emerged into a vast global industry,[5] seeking the latest methods to ensure that businesses adhere to human rights, labor rights, and environmental consciousness. Does any of this activity move us closer to a global community that operates primarily for the common good?

Although the corporate social responsibility movement was growing during the economic expansion of the 1990s, it seems there is less reason to place faith in the ability of the corporate sector to uphold principled values and make meaningful contributions to society, given the Enron fiasco and the rash of corporate accountability scandals that characterized the early years of the twenty-first century. These events, and the decline of various technology corporations, left many skeptical of the 1990's boom, which appears to have been more smoke and mirrors than some realized. The "New Economy," ushered in during the 1990s, provided us with speed and technology that has made many lives easier. However, even during the height of the economic expansion, the global gap in wealth and power, not only persisted, but grew.

The cost of living has skyrocketed, and achieving basic necessities has become increasingly complicated. Technology has transformed basic daily functions, making life easier for most, especially those who are computer literate and have unlimited access to the latest computer equipment. Partly due to technological advances, jobs require higher skills. Lower skilled people could once access manufacturing jobs with consistency, benefits, and overall lifelong possibilities. Today, this same population works in the service sector for significantly less wages and job security.[6] Manufacturing companies have either dissolved or relocated, in search of lower operating costs, leaving workers without jobs.

If those occupying the lower socioeconomic rungs were facing harsher circumstances during boom times, then imagine their status during less stable economic times. Unfortunately, those days have arrived, as layoffs have swept through most industries, and the ranks of the unemployed have ballooned. Job seeking has become a far more stressful, not to mention, protracted endeavor, so much so that the United States federal government extended the period of unemployment benefits (by thirteen weeks) for the recently jobless.

Globalization adds a thick layer of complexity to this picture. Corporations seeking lower operating costs and wages (unimaginable to many in developed countries), can and have relocated, weakening the voice of labor in many cases. Some say low wages in developing countries are inhumane, while others suggest that they are jobs just the same and better than nothing.[7] Whatever the case, low-income communities worldwide have generally not gained advantages from these circumstances. Many multinational corporations operating in the developing world do not face the same regulations governing working conditions, child labor, and the environment, than they would in the United States.[8] Therefore communities in developed countries like the United States lose jobs and stability when corporations leave, and if those companies go to the developing world, these countries only gain limited benefits, as the presence of new jobs may be outweighed by low wages, unhealthy conditions, and various other consequences that can emerge from a far less regulated atmosphere.

The withering boundaries facilitated by globalization are inseparable from an information technology-based economy. Greater communication across borders reduces the relevance of borders in general. One might suggest that easier global communication could foster greater international unity. Activists around the world, for example, have been able to coordinate worldwide protests, most recently seen in the anti-war movement's mass rallies in major cities across the globe of January 18 and February 15, 2003 (among other dates). Essentially, the myriad channels for global communication prove that those who have access to technology and information hold more advantages than ever.

Coupled with globalization, are the increased power and significance of the corporate sector worldwide, and a concurrent decrease in the decision-making power of civil society—communities,[9] despite increased attention to widespread participation and the proliferation of the nonprofit/nongovernmental sector. One of the great challenges in achieving a future where the common good is the first priority is the ability of civil society to assert its potential influence and push major institutions and industries to share power and resources with communities.

Absence of attention to the common good, individual success then becomes the priority, which is driven by personal access to information and resources. Presently, those who have access can corner the market; those who have tended to succeed in doing so have been concentrated in the corporate sector. Even if they are not, their access is still facilitated by resources generated by the private sector. Therefore, our global society must figure out a more effective way to link communities with limited power and access to the resources and information in the corporate sector and the other major institutions and industries in society. The multiple dimensions of the corporate sector traditionally have included finance, technology, media, and various other industries. Moreover, increasingly, other major industries that traditionally have been public ones—such as health care and higher education—have become corporate, as privatization has proliferated.[10]

Some subset of most major industries have explored, to some degree, social responsibility, which has become the means by which various major institutions have engaged in and demonstrated a willingness to partake in actions designed to benefit society, or what I also call, social benefit activity (others may refer to this as "public service," but the term has come to connote specifically government agencies and volunteers). As industries in themselves have developed their own identities and sets of rules and regulations, they have also become defined tightly and ultimately fragmented from the rest of society. Therefore, it is not surprising that these various socially responsible endeavors within particular industries have tended to exist separately from each other. While it is more important than ever for internal movements within particular industries to emerge and challenge their respective fields to play a greater role in improving society, it is equally important to create forums through which cooperation and dialogue across sectors can develop. Without a holistic approach that can transcend these fields, creating a common good is difficult to do.

The interdependence between and among human beings is even more apparent in the relations between industries. The pursuit of a future for everyone, therefore, twofold: closing the gap in power, information, and resources through widespread democratic participation that engages major institutions and industries, and crafting a unique global social movement where cooperation across sector, group, or identity leads to a holistic cry for change that recognizes the interdependency among us all. Neither is an easy task, and both require the crumbling of long-held beliefs and firmly constructed boundaries and hierarchies. The challenge is in understanding the intersection between roles and their relevance to the whole.

A theme such as access to resources and information transcends industry boundaries: Health care, finance, media, the apparel industry, the technology industry, the retail industry, higher education, and various regulated industries all have played a role in limiting access to resources and information. One of our tasks as a global community is to alter this thrust toward equity through creative thinking, leadership, strategy, a willingness to change, social action, and partnership.

The Center for Innovation in Social Responsibility (CISR) at Columbia University was founded with this idea in mind. Through research and dialogue, CISR seeks to improve the impact and significance of social responsibility efforts among various major institutions and industries and link them to a broader democratic pursuit of a common good. An October 26, 2001, Symposium on Social Responsibility was CISR's first attempt to convene a diverse array of practitioners and scholars representing various institutions and industries, to discuss the strengths, weaknesses, and future possibilities for social responsibility efforts. Much of what occurred during this unprecedented event is captured and elaborated upon within these pages. The opinions, ideas, styles, and approaches of the various writers in this volume are reflective of the variation within these multiple fields. Nevertheless, all of these writers have tried to move beyond merely critiquing the state of affairs in each industry and have begun to speculate about solutions. Where are successful case studies that might be emulated elsewhere? What are some untested strategies that might work? What are promising practices that might guide socially responsible efforts and community partnerships?

The challenge of implementing goals within existing global contexts is that we proceed absent of challenging every fundamental dimension of inequality. But the reality is that we must start somewhere. The resources and information within the very institutions that perpetuate structural forms of oppression have the potential to alter inequality.

In trying to envision the necessary steps toward a future for everyone, it is critical to determine if any existing practices can be built upon on the road to progress. A more inclusive and compassionate future requires seeds. One of CISR's objectives is to seek out the seeds that might grow into effective efforts in other spheres. On the one hand, there is plenty of reason to be grim. On the other, we must be committed to finding reasons for hope. Such gems can be found at any level, in any community, and in any sector. The key is to facilitate communication, to create forums that promote dialogue, which can lead to the development of plans that enhance social responsibility.

This view is not promoting charity, with wealthy donors giving and poor recipients receiving. This is about widespread cooperation with shared power and benefit. One of the continually intriguing aspects of the notion of major institutions and industries developing socially responsible initiatives is mutuality. In what ways can large institutions create efforts that are logical extensions of their missions, yet simultaneously beneficial to external constituents? The challenge inherent in this question is the degree to which the interests of a Fortune 500 corporation and a low-income urban community might intersect. We all reside within the same global context, and our actions impact others. To what degree do those interests actually coincide? Much of the literature on corporate social responsibility discusses "win/win" strategies focused on mutual gain, however, the thrust of conclusions in such research tends to emphasize the "business case"[11] for social responsibility, much more than the community case, that is, what do communities gain from partnering with businesses? It would not be wise to assume that communities automatically gain when any major institution or industry decides to focus on social responsibility or partnership, or develop community service programs or philanthropic initiatives. In fact, numerous such programs have faced significant scrutiny for being far more focused on public relations than on actual social change. The truth of such critiques vary by institution; however, companies that are perceived as socially responsible are de facto benefiting from good public relations. The degree to which communities benefit from such initiatives is harder to decipher.

I believe it is important to highlight initiatives where community gain is clear in order to provide a sense of the lessons that can be drawn from socially responsible efforts when implemented in a truly mutually beneficial manner. This is not to suggest that a "business case" is unimportant. In fact, it is far more logical for an institution to engage in a partnership that is an extension of its existing work rather than something that could be seen as extraneous and not a priority. However, the overarching problem is the degree to which an ethos of common good can be found. To what degree is genuine altruism that stresses a greater good over an independent one a present force in business, the law, the media, health care, and so forth? It seems that even with effective social responsibility efforts, it would take some commitment that transcends a business model to create the kind of social change necessary to alter life chances for low-income and disenfranchised communities. Ultimately, this is a question of impact. When we can point to multiple noticeable improvements that were leveraged by socially responsible efforts on the part of major institutions and industries, then we can get a better sense of what is possible. These pages bring out some interesting examples, but it does not feel as if we have reached the point where a great deal can be expected in terms of extensive societal improvements. Reaching that point will require a great deal of work, difficult conversations, and leadership that places the common good at the center.

In my own observations of projects involving some degree of cooperation between communities and large institutions, power dynamics persist, even in the more effective, well-meaning cases.[12] The entire field of institutions and industries grappling with social responsibility and community partnerships must confront their willingness to shift the power balance, and actually *change as institutions*. This could be a tall order for this generation, but what about the next one? The creative solutions necessary to forge a genuine commitment to equity at the highest levels may very well rest with the next generation, underscoring the importance of training and development with an eye toward the future. To what degree are communal values and a sense of social responsibility incorporated into education? In what ways are professional schools training a new generation willing to challenge insufficient and unethical practices in their respective fields?

In reflecting upon the potential of social responsibility efforts and community partnerships, it is important to delineate the realm of possibility. In thinking about inequality, it becomes clear that the world's major institutions and industries wield control over two key areas: *resources* and *information*. Therefore, access by the general population to these areas is ultimately in the hands of those who command major institutions and industries. In other words, institutions of higher education, corporations, the legal system, the health care industry, and the media all control access to valuable information and resources. Oftentimes, the quality of what can be accessed depends upon price—laws of supply and demand. But it appears that the principle difficulty with this model is that one generally requires a certain degree of information and resources to begin with in order to achieve greater access. Of course, this is how we can see generations in poverty or generations in wealth. Therefore, a longer term quest for the social responsibility movement should be to democratize information and resources—to free up access.

The area of *resources* includes the goods created by corporations, natural resources in the environment, and currency itself. The area of *information* is far more complex, yet increasingly critical, as the "knowledge-based" economy continues to evolve. The services from professionals, technology, and education have become increasingly central in accessing resources. In some ways, this has had a democratizing effect for a few, who were able to sell their knowledge to achieve levels of resources that far surpassed their previous generations. However, as the dot-com revolution began to crumble, it was the older "blue chip" companies with preexisting resources that were able ultimately to capitalize on the preeminence of information and technology.

Even outside of technology, information has secured incredible power. The proliferation of consultants and "agents" involved in every concept under the sun has demonstrated the potential of individuals to acquire information and sell it, in turn. Another great power of information lies in the shaping of ideas, public opinion, and popular priorities. Among the most accessible means of information are newspapers, magazines, television, and radio. Despite the proliferation of alternative media, the popular media still plays a central role; it is the most accessible media, therefore its content is critical. One salient trend has been the consolidation of control of the popular media, which enables narrow perspectives to dominate the content of multiple media outlets—all different, yet relatively the same.[13]

In looking at the power of the media, the concept of control becomes very apparent. For communities, therefore, the issue is access, but ultimately, if access is continually denied, the real issue is control. Through partnership, the social responsibility movement may have the potential to both increase access as well as control. While many have feared the idea of a zero sum game that suggests what is good for the powerful is bad for the powerless, it is possible that the concept of partnership between major institutions/industries and communities is a third way to work across boundaries toward a common good.

The idea of community engagement in decision making has gained some credence in government and in the nonprofit sector. The community building movement has strongly emphasized bottom up community planning and governance.[14] A concept called "community lawyering" has emerged in the legal field.[15] The entire discussion around the civic responsibility of higher education has stressed the notion of colleges and universities as promoters of democracy for students, but they also need to work in partnership with communities.[16] The health care industry has come under some scrutiny for its distance from patients. Some suggest that greater communication between caregivers and patients leads to better health care.[17] While the mass media has remained controlled by a few powerful corporations, a community media movement has encouraged residents to present the issues of importance to them through their own avenues.[18] The notion of the poor and disadvantaged as recipients of service rather than as active participants alongside social workers has been criticized roundly.

Another important concept within the social responsibility movement is human rights. Often directly tied to relative control, the kinds of abuses by multinational corporations around child labor and working conditions has been under the spotlight, especially with respect to the apparel industry and the sweatshops of the twenty-first century. In these cases, corporations take advantage of communities that lack control as well as access to resources and information, thus violating their human rights.[19] Indeed, it is often the case that disenfranchised communities are vulnerable to a point where their human rights can be violated as a result of limited options.

It still holds true that the communities with the least access and control must organize in order to bring about change that improves their lives. But must that organizing always be in isolation? Are there ways in which communities and local industry can join forces? Certainly not in all instances, but in some areas such collaboration might be possible. In putting together this collection of essays, we seek that level of common ground by bringing together the work of practitioners and scholars to build upon successful models that prioritize community gain and governance.

No approach discussed in these pages is perfect, but the diverse perspectives and case studies provide some basis to key concerns when seeking to improve the social responsibility and community impact of major institutions and industries. What may be most useful about this book is that the ways in which various types of institutions and industries have dealt with these issues are all discussed in under one cover. This book is not about how one industry has addressed social responsibility; it is about resources, information, access, and control, beyond boundaries, and the degree to which various fields have explored efforts to reach common ground with communities, as well as the efforts of communities to maximize their dealings with major institutions and industries.

This book has three sections: Part I. A Corporate Environment in Transition? Part II. Case Studies and the Philanthropic Paradox, and Part III. Ideas and Information: Power and Access. The first part, A Corporate Environment in Transition? is so titled due to the decades of growth by the corporate social responsibility movement and the simultaneous consolidation of corporate power, not to mention the recent revelations of corporate corruption. Some of these chapters were written before Enron and fellow fiscal wizards became national scandals. Nevertheless, they provide a sense of the state of corporate social responsibility and some of the key concerns looking forward.

In chapter 1, Jonathan Cohen thoroughly captures the global landscape of corporate social responsibility and addresses the increased attention to greater corporate accountability exhibited through the development of various recent initiatives, including the sweeping Global Compact championed by Secretary General of the United Nations Kofi Annan. In chapter 2, Osagie Kingsley Obasogie addresses the public/private distinction in the legal field and the degree to which this allows lawyers in the private interest area to advocate at the expense of community needs. He uses an analysis of such dynamics within the legal profession as a springboard to recommend limiting the public/ private distinction in order to incorporate social responsibility in all spheres of life and enable the next generation to forge careers that uphold the public interest regardless of their chosen type of work. Finally, in chapter 3, Frank Dixon indicates how effective performance in environmental responsibility can improve corporate performance and explores the complexities involved in measuring such a correlation.

In the part II, Case Studies and the Philanthropic Paradox, we include some concrete case studies of social responsibility efforts. Also of note in this section is the discussion of the role of foundations, which are often overlooked as major institutions unto themselves. Because of their explicit social missions, large foundations, in particular, sometimes escape the kind of scrutiny that might confront similar sized institutions in the private sector.[20] Some writing about methods for more effective or "responsive" philanthropy has emerged.[21] Additionally, this section discusses the concept of intermediary organizations, often medium-sized nonprofit organizations responsible for leveraging access to resources and information for low-income and disenfranchised communities.

Allan J. Formicola, Walid Michelen, and Sandra Harris in chapter 4, discuss a case study sponsored by the Kellogg Foundation, designed to provide intensive access to health care in low-income communities nationwide through partnerships with hospitals and universities. In chapter 5, Carol Glazer explores a unique partnership between a major retail development corporation and a foundation, capturing its successes and many challenges along the way. Partnerships of this sort can be quite instructive in terms of leveraging the assets of different types of major institutions on behalf of low-income communities. Aida Rodriguez, Joseph A. Pereira, and Shana Brodnax in chapter 6, provide an overview of the challenges facing nonprofit organizations and the types of assistance provided by intermediary organizations in order to meet those needs. Although the services are in place, the authors maintain that the access of nonprofits to these services could be improved. Finally, in chapter 7,

Perry Mehrling questions the continuous pursuit by large foundations of expansive endowments and the limited expectations for
those funds to reach communities. As foundations are only required
by law to "pay out" 5 percent of their assets per year, Mehrling suggests that these institutions are allowed to exist more for their own
perpetuity than their responsibility to the public.

In the part III, Ideas and Information: Power and Access, we hone
in on the various aspects of an information-based economy, from
higher education to technology to the media to the law. Providing
both examples and analysis, this section explores the possibilities for
communities to take advantage of existing informational resources
and draws conclusions about the transition of socially responsible
values to the next generation.

Tyshammie Cooper, in chapter 8, discusses how technology has
pervaded all that we do, including our access to information, making
computer literacy more essential than ever. The persistence of a digital divide has exacerbated preexisting power dynamics, however, a
number of efforts have been instituted to close the gap. A challenge to
these efforts is that low-income communities often don't possess the
basic literacy to be able to learn certain aspects of computer usage. In
chapter 9, Heather Bent Tamir ponders the role of the media in shaping public opinion and identifies strategies that can help communities
and nonprofit organizations leverage access to the media for social
justice aims. She particularly notes some of the accomplishments of
her employer, PolicyLink, which established a media office within its
overall policy and research tent. In chapter 10, David N. Cox and
Melissa Pearce evaluate the extent to which higher education has
been able to create viable initiatives that further the higher educational mission and improve communities. The process by which institutions of higher education and communities engage in partnership,
they maintain, leads to the creation of new knowledge.

From the preceding chapters, the role of government and the nonprofit sector emerges as an essential element in bridging the chasm
between communities and major institutions/industries. As the clos-
est potential representative of civil society voices, the nonprofit sector, in particular, must also increase its level of engagement if we are
to truly be able to create a future for everyone.

Abbreviations

AACU	American Association of Colleges and Universities
AAHE	American Association of Higher Education
AASCU	American Association of State College (or Colleges) and Universities
ACHEP	Association for Community-Higher Education Partnership
ASNE	American Society of Newspaper Editors
CAPHE	Consortium for the Advancement of Private Higher Education
CCPH	Campus-Community Partnerships for Health
CDCs	community development corporations
CEA	Community Employment Alliance
CERCLA	Comprehensive Environmental Response, Compensation, and Liability Act
CHIP	Children's Health Insurance Program
CIC	Council of Independent Colleges
CISR	Center for Innovation in Social Responsibility
CJR	*Columbia Journalism Review*
COPC	Community Outreach Partnership Center
CRA	Community Reinvestment Act
CSH	Corporation for Supportive Housing
CTCNet	Community Technology Centers' Network
DJSI World	Dow Jones Sustainability World Indexes

EMS	environment management systems
EPA	Environmental Protection Agency
ERNS	Emergency Response Notification System
FCC	Federal Communications Commission
FLA	Fair Labor Association
FTA	Federal Transit Authority
HEI	higher education institution
HELP	Hispanic Enterprises Launching Programs
HIP	Hispanics in Philanthropy
HIV/AIDS	Human Immunodeficiency Virus/Acquired Immune Deficiency Syndrome
IRAAS	Institute for Research in African American Studies
LISC	Local Initiatives Support Corporation
NASULGC	National Association of State Universities and Land Grant Colleges
NCCED	National Congress on Community Economic Development
NCCUP	National Consortium for Community-University Partnerships
NCDI	National Community Development Initiative
NEDLC	National Economic Development and Law Center
NGOs	non-governmental organizations
NMCVC	Northern Manhattan Community Voices Collaborative
N-PAC	Non-Profit Assistance Corporation
PMA	Pharmaceutical Manufacturers' Association
PM & M	Performance Measurement and Management
PRLDEF	Puerto Rican Legal Defense Fund
ODI	Organizational Development Initiative
RCRA	Resource Conservation and Recovery Act
RFPs	request for proposals
SEC	Securities and Exchange Commission
SMEs	small- and medium-sized enterprises
SRB	Socially Responsible Business
SRI	socially responsible investing
TEF	The Enterprise Foundation
TRI	toxic release inventory
UNITE	Union of Needletrades, Industrial and Textile Employees
WTO	World Trade Organization

Part I

A Corporate Environment in Transition?

SOCIALLY RESPONSIBLE BUSINESS

Global Trends

JONATHAN COHEN

The fast growing field of socially responsible business is difficult to keep up with due to the increasing interconnectedness between business, government, and the non-governmental sectors of society.[1] The walls between the three are blurring as the boundaries between the issues of the day and geography are increasingly coming together. While business, the flow of capital, non-governmental organizations (NGOs), and information increasingly have become global in the post–cold war world, governments have retained their national focus, losing ground as a result. This has produced a pressing need for new solutions that respond to new demands for accountability and access from all corners of the globe.

This chapter provides a survey of global trends in socially responsible business and aims to make sense of disparate yet interconnected societal changes. A current picture of global trends in socially responsible business starts with the impact of September 11. From there the coverage turns to recent global trends, notably the United Nation's new relationship with business, also known as the Global Compact. Subsequently, the increasing number of multistakeholder partnerships between the for-profit, public, and non-governmental sectors of society are examined with a particular focus on the battle over life-saving drugs. The declining but still powerful role of government to shape business behavior through enforcement of intellectual property rights and in response to problems in the extractive industries is examined as well as the quintessential role of NGO pressure on socially responsible business. Socially responsible investing (SRI) and shareholder advocacy are examined in light of current trends, and finally the intellectual development of the field is described in the final section.

September 11

It has been said that everything changed after September 11, 2001, and the global prospects of socially responsible business is no exception. The twice-targeted twin towners of the World Trade Center represented the American center of global business incarnate. The reaction to the subsequent retaliation bombing of Afghanistan was telling. McDonald's restaurants burned in Pakistan. The *New York Times* reported on October 14 that mobs targeted Nike stores, Pizza Huts, Dunkin' Donuts, and even billboards advertising Coca-Cola, Pepsi, Kentucky Fried Chicken, and others—the most visible, and accessible, symbols of the United States. Fox News reported on October 19 that a Muslim group in India, the country with the second largest Muslim population on earth after Indonesia, announced a boycott of U.S. goods, including Coca-Cola, until the U.S. bombing in Afghanistan stops.

Global brands are so recognizable that they are increasingly the target of hatred by the disaffected, not only the target of desire by consumers. As with other socially responsible business trends, global brands faced the firing line independently of September 11. When the United States retaliated against France for banning hormone-laden beef, José Bové and the French Farmers' Confederation garnered global media attention by "strategically dismantling" a McDonald's, Naomi Klein wrote in *The Nation* on October 22. Then there is the now famous spate of plate glass window smashing of Starbucks shops in Seattle during the World Trade Organization (WTO) protests in 1999. Global brands serve on the front lines in the globalization culture wars, and they can expect to see more action in the years ahead.

The flip side to this situation lies in the larger search for meaning that America in particular is now going through. If a newfound appreciation for faith and family is not just a passing phenomenon, then in all likelihood business will face a greater emphasis on the spiritual in the workplace. In fact, this has already been happening in the business world. Almost a dozen conferences on business and spirituality occurred in the United States alone in 1998, along with two work and spirituality focused journals, and an increase in spiritual practices, with meditation foremost among them.[2] The International Conference on Business and Consciousness will hold its seventh such event in 2002. This interest stretches beyond the United States, to Japan, and somewhat less to Australia as well. And what is the most widely printed new topic among business school texts? Spirituality and business leadership.[3] The combination of the preexisting trend of spirituality and business with the apocalyptic overtones of September 11 add up to a potentially far-reaching impact on business behavior.

How this focus influences bottom line business decisions remains to be seen, however. The tension tearing at the reality of Socially Responsible Business (SRB) in the post–September 11 world is best represented by two oft-repeated refrains in the event's immediate aftermath. On one hand, we heard that there is more to life than just work, and that values and faith are more important than ever before. On the other, the economic slowdown that was in the works prior to the terrorist attacks and accelerated as a result of them, breeds hard economic decisions. If the immediate reaction to the September 11 terrorist attacks is any indication—massive layoffs by corporations before the dust had even cleared in downtown Manhattan, including a brazen attempt to avoid severance pay by one airline, as well as the great bailout rush— the precepts of socially responsible business will be tested.

Television executives, for example, are now open to accepting advertisements for hard liquor for the first time in over fifty years, according to a report in the *Wall Street Journal* on October 4, 2001. Alcohol producers decided that the time was right to scrap their voluntary ban on television advertising that they self-imposed in 1948, just as television executives faced steep declines in advertising revenue. What's a desperate company to do? How bad does it have to get before values and ethics are thrown out the window? How strong are the values of business? The BBC reported on October 19, 2001, that a string of gloomy outlooks were projected for the world's biggest economies in 2001 and the Organization for Economic Co-operation and Development and the World Bank, which portends a true test of faith for global business, concurred for 2002.

On the positive side, the corporate community demonstrated its philanthropic generosity by giving tens of millions of dollars to September 11 charity funds. One only need look at the United Way web site, for example, to find a long laundry list of sizeable corporate donations.[4] Consumers can certainly look forward to an increase in cause-related marketing. A greater emphasis on equating the notion of consumer spending on such products, especially during an economic downturn, as being equivalent to charity can be expected as well. Hopefully, businesses will turn to measures that go beyond the strictly philanthropic and impact their operational side beyond those that involve security. Business, like everything else, will surely be changed permanently by the events of September 11.

United Nations Global Compact

Another watershed moment in recent history that marked a turning point in the evolution of socially responsible business was the 1999 WTO protests in Seattle. Unlike September 11, however, this event was predicted in advance. In the words of then–Assistant Secretary General John Ruggie, "When [the United Nations] Secretary-General [and recent Nobel peace prize winner] Kofi Annan first proposed the Global Compact in January 1999, he stated categorically that globalization, as we knew it, was not sustainable. Indeed, he predicted precisely the kind of backlash that hit ten months later in Seattle and in various venues since.[5] The concept of socially responsible business is inherently universal and consequently requires a universal institution as its champion.

The Global Compact provides a framework through which the U.N. can engage with business in the areas of human rights, labor standards, and environmental practices. These three issues were chosen because they are "the areas in which universal values have already been defined by international agreements, including the Universal

Declaration of Human Rights, the International Labor Organization's Declaration on Fundamental Principles and Rights at Work, and the Rio Declaration of the United Nations Conference on Environment and Development."[6]

U.N. strengths in promoting corporate citizenship include a global constituency, reach, and network of agencies, an all-encompassing progressive mission, vast communications vehicles in the world's major languages, and credibility, particularly with the developing world. U.N. challenges in promoting corporate citizenship include establishing policies that all of its agencies embrace, including reaching out to small- and medium-sized enterprises (SMEs), approaching partnerships with business as more than opportunities to supplement funding by governments and screening criteria.

Partnerships between the U.N. and business have the potential to positively alter the face of globalization, however, collaboration with business could open the U.N. to criticism of helping to whitewash poor corporate reputations if its relations with business are not engaged in carefully. The U.N. has a weak normative framework with regard to business. While a body of rules governing relations with NGOs has been developed over the course of the U.N.'s lifespan, starting with Article 71 of the U.N. Charter, a similar body of rules concerning the private sector is lacking.[7] NGOs apply for formal consultative status with U.N. bodies. Over one thousand five hundred NGOs have such status with the U.N. Economic and Social Council and more than one thousand six hundred with the Department of Public Information, for example.[8]

A greater understanding is needed by NGOs, and American businesses in particular, that the U.N. Global Compact is not a code of conduct, like SA8000 or the Marine Stewardship Council. While the U.N. must establish a policy to deal with companies that do not abide by the Global Compact, NGOs must also take a lead role in holding companies to their commitments. This is in fact starting to happen. The Institute for Agriculture and Trade Policy published a scathing report in June 2001, for example, that cited the company Aventis for violating the seventh Global Compact principle concerning "a precautionary approach to environmental challenges." The company's genetically engineered StarLink™ corn illegally contaminated the U.S. food supply and seed stock.[9]

Aventis moved StarLink™ to market without the benefit of long-term studies to determine whether it was safe, and it should not have done so. Aventis also failed to abide by the U.N. guideline for applying the precautionary approach to "communicate with stakeholders." The company was legally required to inform growers that StarLink corn cannot be sold into international or human food markets and that a 660-foot buffer zone must be planted, but did not take steps to ensure this was done effectively. Having been released into the environment, StarLink™ is now impossible to recall. After the scandal broke, Aventis attempted to control the damage by avoiding responsibility and trying to obtain retroactive approval. The U.N.'s reaction to Aventis and cases like it will point toward what can be expected realistically from the organization when it comes to companies that do not abide by their commitments to Global Compact principles. This is important because companies whose behavior are starkly at odds with the Global Compact principles undermine the program as a whole and its potential to grow into a positive force.[10]

The growth of the U.N. Global Compact has been impressive to date with the involvement of several hundred companies from all regions of the world, with more in the pipeline, from a start of under fifty at the time of the program's launch on July 26, 2000. The U.N. has undertaken a road show to make the Compact truly global—and local. Senior contacts from all sectors in Brazil, China, Ghana, India, Indonesia, Lebanon, Pakistan, Poland, Russia, South Africa, Thailand, Sweden, and elsewhere have taken part, with more countries to come. Partnership projects have been set up involving companies, civil society, and governments in reducing poverty and in developing human capital. The Global Compact Learning Forum, a mechanism by which companies post summaries of their actions in support of the Global Compact principles to the program's web site, is poised to go "live" at the time of this writing, and will go a long way toward demonstrating what the program is capable of accomplishing.[11]

Some sixty representatives from the public, private, and non-governmental sectors addressed the subject of business operations in parts of the world that feature armed conflict at the Global Compact's first Policy Dialogue session in New York on March 21–22, 2001. This issue was chosen first for a reason. Some of the most contentious business activity occurs in these zones of conflict, particularly in regard to the extractive industries, such as diamonds, oil, and believe it or not, even chocolate. "Conflict diamonds" originate from territory controlled by forces opposed to legitimate and internationally recognized governments that are used to fund military action in opposition to those governments. On December 1, 2000, the U.N. General Assembly, recognizing that conflict diamonds are a crucial factor in prolonging brutal wars in parts of Africa, unanimously adopted a resolution against the role of illicit diamonds in fueling armed conflict.[12]

The White House issued an Executive Order on May 23, 2001, that cites the role of the illicit diamond trade in funding the insurgent Revolutionary United Front's operations in the civil war in Sierra Leone. Further, the Executive Order prohibits the importation into the United States of all rough diamonds from Sierra Leone except for those importations controlled through a Certificate of Origin regime of the government of Sierra Leone.[13] The diamond trade points to the fact that international flashpoints increasingly can involve causes related to the private sector.

The same is true for the oil industry. When attempting to resolve the long civil war in Angola recently, for example, who did the U.N. secretary general send his envoy to meet with in February 2001? Oil companies. The U.N. Undersecretary General for Africa Ibrahim Gambari said oil companies operating in Angola could contribute to peace efforts because they have "leverage on the government," adding that "the government will listen to them."[14] The question remains whether corporations will act on the same motivations for working with the U.N. as they did before September 11. Transnational companies with operations that reach the developing world will need the U.N. more than ever because of September 11. The U.N.'s credibility with the masses, rather than governments, in the developing world stands as a strength in its work with business now and for the future.

Partnerships

Partnerships between the for-profit, public, and non-governmental sectors are a consequence of a decline in governmental power and corresponding growth in business and non-governmental power, particularly in the post–cold war era. As government has increasingly proven unwilling or unable to curb the negative aspects of global business expansionism, NGOs have moved away from calling for public regulation of the private sector. Instead they have actively sought direct solutions to these problems, which has entailed working in partnership with business, often their former adversary.[15] The term for this failure of government is civil regulation.[16]

A major socially responsible business battle took place in 2001 over access to life-saving drugs. The epic life versus profit struggle in the first half of the year centered on access to HIV/AIDS drugs in the developing economy of South Africa. The Pharmaceutical Manufacturers' Association of South Africa (PMA) representing thirty-nine leading drug companies brought a court case against the South African government's 1997 Medicines Act, in an effort to prevent the country from importing cheap alternatives to branded medicines.[17] A confluence of a dire health crisis, business stonewalling, NGO campaigning, and efforts from intergovernmental agencies such as the U.N. World Health Organization and UNAIDS, and of course media coverage, forced the issue to a head. The issue in this case pitted intellectual property rights in the form of drug patents against some 25 million people with AIDS in Africa and 4.7 million AIDS sufferers in South Africa.

The drug companies sought to recoup millions of dollars and years of research invested in developing their drugs. If South Africa were allowed to import cheaper, generic versions of HIV/AIDS drugs in violation of patents, then what would stop other countries from importing generic versions of patented drugs? What incentive would the companies have to invest in the drugs in the first place? The drug companies failed to grasp the exceptional stakes involved and consequently held tightly to a blind faith in the right to profit regardless of the circumstance. Missing the opportunity to work cooperatively with stakeholders such as the South African government, the U.N.,

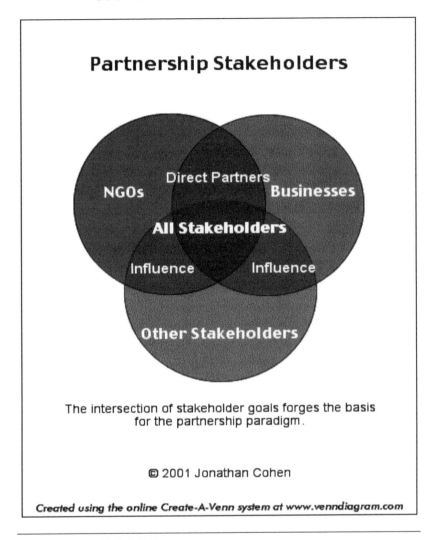

Figure 1.1 Partnership Stakeholders

and NGOs, the companies were brought to heel in the most public and humiliating of manners. It is precisely the intersection of interests between such stakeholders that forms the basis for partnerships.

The U.N. Security Council had already declared HIV/AIDS to be a threat to international security.[18] Oxfam, the Treatment Action Campaign, and Medecins Sans Frontieres, along with many other organizations, campaigned tirelessly to get the drug companies to drop their case. Some 250,000 people signed a protest petition that was presented to the PMA.[19] In April 2001, U.N. Secretary General Kofi Annan issued a call to action for the creation of a Global Fund to fight HIV/AIDS. Media attention buzzed incessantly. The world's attention would soon be focused on the subject at the June 2001 U.N. General Assembly Special Session on HIV/AIDS. With the pressure mounting, the PMA buckled in April 2001 and dropped their court case against the South African government and allowed the country to import generic drugs. Subsequently, the fund the secretary general called for came into being as the Global Fund to Fight AIDS, Tuberculosis & Malaria, and consisted of over forty representatives drawn from developing and developed countries, NGOs, U.N. agencies, foundations, and members of the private sector.[20] This type of intersectoral tension and collaboration has also been evident concerning intellectual property rights, extractive industries, and sweatshop labor.

Government

As if the drug industry did not face a titanic situation in the gradual build up to the apex of the HIV/AIDS drug war in the spring of 2001, it was confronted with a military war after September 11 and demand anew for drug patents to be set aside in the fall of 2001. This time the drug in demand was Cipro and the countries were not South Africa or Brazil, but Canada, and that bastion of free market capitalism and unyielding defender of patents and the rule of law—the United States. The company in the spotlight was Bayer, whose unstinting withholding of its drug and assertion of the dominance of intellectual property rights sounded eerily familiar to HIV/AIDS drugs in South Africa.

Only when the Canadian government ignored Bayer's patent and asked a Toronto company to supply 1 million Cipro pills did the company, the sole patent holder of the drug, insist it could meet the government's needs. Bayer offered Cipro to the United States at its usual government price. The United States demanded it at about half that price. Again, Bayer failed to grasp the exceptional stakes involved and held too tightly to a blind faith in the right to profit regardless of the circumstance. The result has proven to be the unthinkable—the Health and Human Services Secretary of the United States of America, Tommy G. Thompson, went to the press and threatened to violate Bayer's patent if the company did not come around. The result should never have been in doubt.[21]

Another groundbreaking example of the role government can play with regard to business behavior occurred on December 20, 2000, when the U.S. and British governments, several major multinational corporations, business organizations, international human rights groups, and unions agreed on a set of voluntary principles on security and human rights in the oil, gas, and mining industries. The agreement was announced jointly by the U.S. Department of State and Britain's Foreign and Commonwealth Office. Specifically, the principles focused on the relationship between the extractive industries and private and public security forces in maintaining the safety and security of their operations. Risk assessment and responses to human rights abuses were included as well.[22]

Less than ten months later another high-profile multistakeholder partnership with an extractive industry of a different sort was formed. As if we needed another reason to feel guilty about eating chocolate, global chocolate manufacturers and members of the U.S. Congress announced on October 1, 2001, a comprehensive plan to address child slavery on West African cocoa farms and in the cocoa-chocolate sector worldwide. The agreement has been endorsed by the U.N. International Labor Organization, NGOs, the International Cocoa Organization—a trade organization, and others.[23] The agreement calls for global, industrywide standards and independent monitoring, reporting and public certification to identify and eliminate forced and slave child labor in the growing and processing of cocoa beans. Public certification that cocoa used in chocolate or related products has been grown and processed without child labor also constitutes the agreement. Who will define and enforce the standards for this effort and ensure compliance? A public-private sector partnership will act as the definitive authority and will encompass NGOs with expertise in child labor as well as industry.[24] The chocolate industry may have learned what not to do from the drug industry.

The chocolate industry likely learned what to do from an earlier high-profile example of a multistakeholder partnership involving government that took place in the aftermath of the Kathie Lee Gifford sweatshop scandal in April 1996. The White House convened apparel companies, labor unions, and other NGOs to discuss the need for labor standards that could combat sweatshops. The apparel industry was represented by businesses such as Liz Claiborne, L.L. Bean, and Nike. Unions and groups such as the National Consumers League and the Lawyers Committee for Human Rights were involved along with academia. The partners released an agreement in April 1997 that included a "Workplace Code of Conduct" and "Principles of Monitoring" for the apparel industry.[25]

Issues addressed in the code included forced and child labor, workplace discrimination, health and safety, freedom of association and collective bargaining, hours of work, and of course salary and benefits. The principles called for companies to establish written standards for the workplace, monitor compliance with the standards, collect data on and audit the monitoring, ask for information concerning compliance from interested stakeholders, and set up a remediation process. Independent external monitors were to conduct inspections of a sampling of company and contractor facilities with total access and report on the findings as well as make recommendations.[26]

The partnership partially broke up, however, due to a fundamental disagreement over a key aspect of the negotiations concerning goals in 1998. Key players—the garment workers' union UNITE and the Retail, Wholesale and Department Store Union as well as the Interfaith Center for Corporate Responsibility—dropped out of the partnership negotiations following a disagreement over the idea of a living wage, or a wage that meets basic human needs as opposed to a minimum wage, a higher percentage of factories that would be externally monitored, and operations in countries with poor labor rights records. A more moderate but less representative group survived. The remaining partners established an NGO, the Fair Labor Association (FLA), to carry out the agreements that would allow companies in good standing to use the FLA symbol on products and in advertising.[27]

Non-industry stakeholders considered some aspects of the goals that dealt with monitoring to be weak, however. Only 10 percent of manufacturing facilities, for example, are monitored annually for the first three years, with as little as 5 percent after that. Questions have also been raised about the acceptable number of hours worked in a week as well as overtime allowed.[28] The partners that left over the living wage issue did not achieve all of their goals, but they did succeed in obtaining recognition of the right to freedom of association and collective bargaining under the code. Students, human rights groups, and labor unions that believed the FLA did not go far enough formed a separate organization, the Worker Rights Consortium, which has instituted more stringent labor standards.

NGO Pressure

Non-governmental pressure has been the driving force behind the rise in socially responsible business and civil regulation. The immediate aftermath of September 11 had a profound effect on the insistent and at times unruly public conscience known as the non-governmental sector. For example, a group dedicated to the issue of climate change that called itself Families Against Bush posted the following message on its web site sometime after September 11:

> [Families Against Bush] is suspending active campaigning against the climate position of the U.S. Administration out of respect for, sympathy and solidarity with the people of the USA.
>
> We will also consider changing the name FAB if that is widely supported.

A much more prominent group, the 600,000–member Sierra Club, announced on September 12 that it had suspended campaigning in response to September 11 terrorist attacks:

> Now is a time for mourning, for reflection and for solutions to the immediate crisis at hand. Our nation faces other long-term problems and challenges, but now is not the time for those debates. Only when the healing is underway and we have begun tackling the security challenges we face, will our nation be ready to focus again on other issues. When the focus returns to other longer-term issues, the Sierra Club will resume our national debate on those issues.[29]

In the new post–September 11 reality that will not tolerate violent dissent, the anti-globalization movement known as the Black Block—made up of radical anarchist, Starbucks window smashing, black bandana wearing protesters—will become marginalized. There can be no equivocating on the part of legitimate groups that such violence has no place in their movement. Organizations that mix anti–U.S. and anti-war on terrorism messages with their anti-globalization efforts will find the campaigning terrain all rocky and uphill. Differences between those that seek to humanize globalization and those that oppose it outright will likely fester.

The World Economic Forum in New York in early 2002 provided the first glimpse of how NGOs plan to protest at the ongoing series of international meetings that serve as the backdrop to popular expressions of discontent with the status quo. Peaceful protesters won out in the first round, although their numbers were limited due to a blanket security presence. Increased civil liberties questions, which marked the governmental response, can be counted on at future demonstrations as well.[30]

Predictions of the movement's demise are overstated, however.[31] NGOs will need to protect their most effective tactic to change business behavior—the publicity campaign.[32] The ground rules have changed. While NGOs are not going anywhere, the part of the movement that has engaged in direct action protest will likely lose ground to the part that works in the boardroom.

Socially Responsible Investing

The boardroom leads us to another crucial international trend, socially responsible investing. Once thought of as the domain of granola chewing hippies that hadn't gotten over Vietnam, socially responsible investing in the United States topped the two TRILLION dollar mark in 1999. That amounts to one out of every $8 under management being invested responsibly and represents an 82 percent increase from 1997 levels. The number of screened socially responsible mutual funds increased to 175 from 139, which itself was an increase from just 55 in 1995. Social investors involved in shareholder advocacy actively worked with companies to encourage greater corporate social responsibility, which was made easier by virtue of their control of nearly a trillion dollars.[33]

The fastest growing component of socially responsible investing has been portfolios that both screen and engage in shareholder advocacy. Assets in portfolios utilizing both strategies grew 215 percent, from $84 billion in 1997 to $265 billion in 1999. Tobacco topped the list of issues screened by social investors, with an almost universal 96 percent rate of avoidance by socially screened portfolios. After tobacco, the majority of assets screened were for gambling (86 percent), alcohol (83 percent), weapons (81 percent), and the environment (79 percent). Other screens include human rights (43 percent), labor issues (38 percent), birth control/abortion (23 percent), and animal welfare (15 percent).[34]

Another key development in the SRI field has been the establishment of the Dow Jones Sustainability Indexes (DJSI), which are the first global indexes that track the performance of sustainability-driven companies, representing sixty-two industries worldwide. Companies included on the DJSI World are recognized as being the top 10 percent in corporate sustainability and are leading their industries by setting standards for best practices and demonstrating superior environmental, social, and economic performances. Those listed on the DJSI World are chosen from 2,500 of the largest capitalized companies in the Dow Jones Global Index.[35]

Intellectual Development of the SRB Field

The maturation of the SRB field as evidenced by its penetration of the Dow Jones, also reflects an intellectual development of the field. Recently, an important periodical was launched called the *Journal of Corporate Citizenship*. The impressive number and quality of books being published in the field in 2001 alone includes *Perspectives on Corporate Citizenship* (edited by Joerg Andriof and Malcolm McIntosh, Greenleaf Publishing, 2001); *The Civil Corporation, The New Economy of Corporate Citizenship* (Simon Zadek, Earthscan, 2001); *The Business of Social Responsibility* (Harsh Shrivastava and Shankar Venkateswaran, Partners in Change, 2001); *Leading Corporate Citizens: Vision, Values, Value Added* (Sandra Waddock, McGraw-Hill, 2001); *A Public Role for the Private Sector: Industry Self-Regulation in a*

Global Economy (Virginia Haufler, Carnegie Endowment for International Peace, 2001); *SA8000, The Definitive Guide* (Financial Times Prentice Hall, 2001); *Beyond the Campus: How Colleges and Universities Form Partnerships with their Communities* (David Maurrasse, Routledge, 2001); also, publishing houses such as Greenleaf in England are proving to be crucial intellectual hubs of new thinking in the field.

A similar development has taken place within the ivory tower. Eighty-two MBA programs worldwide now report including social and environmental topics, according to the annual *Beyond Grey Pinstripes* business school survey. The survey also finds, however, that such issues are ghettoized outside of core curriculum into ethics classes, volunteer, and philanthropic activities. Also, environmental topics are generally taught in stand-alone electives rather than linked to core business strategy. Notably, students who want to learn these subjects give MBA programs the pathetic grade of "D+" concerning the frequency with which social and environmental issues are raised by faculty in required courses.[36]

While business schools have increasingly added SRB course work, some have even established entire arms that conduct academic work in addition to work with companies on these issues. However, these arms are not without their own financing needs. Take, for example the Nottingham University Business School's International Centre for Corporate Social Responsibility. The Centre's stated aims are to study the social and environmental responsibilities of multinational companies to the communities in which they operate. Initial funding announced for staff and for student scholarships within the new Centre included £3.8 million, phased over three years, from British American *Tobacco*, hardly the most socially responsible of funding sources.[37] Consequently, the Centre appeared compromised before it even began operation.

Likewise, the University of Warwick's Corporate Citizenship Unit in the U.K. is supported by a Consortium of Business Partners, who have made long-term commitments to provide core funding to the unit, which includes the Mining and Energy Research Network. Partners include BP Amoco and Rio Tinto plc, an oil company and a mining company. Dependence on financing from companies in the very sector an academic institution is set up to research gives the appearance of a stacked deck.

Conclusion

Key international trends in socially responsible business include the aftermath of September 11, the U.N. Global Compact, multistakeholder partnerships, the declining, but still powerful role of government, NGO pressure, socially responsible investing, and finally the intellectual development of the field.

There are *many* other issues that are not included here that fall under the heading of international trends in SRB, including trade, transparency, tobacco, and corporate reporting, among others. The U.S.–Jordanian trade pact announced on October 24, 2000, was the first ever to have, in the body of a U.S. trade agreement itself, key provisions that firmly link free trade and the protection of the environment and of workers' rights.[38] The Transparency International Corruption Perceptions Index, which ranks countries in terms of the degree to which corruption is perceived to exist between public officials and politicians, has become a powerful global anti-corruption tool.[39] The embattled tobacco industry has taken the fight to the U.N. World Health Organization, which released a report on August 2, 2000, with the title "Tobacco Company Strategies to Undermine Tobacco Control Activities at the World Health Organization."[40] More than one thousand participants representing hundreds of organizations have come to be involved in the Global Reporting Initiative, which is open to all individuals and organizations interested in sustainability reporting.[41]

September 11 has hardened the global focus on business activities, which were after all the overt target of the terrorist attacks. While corporate philanthropy has been strengthened at least in the short term, the mettle of business values will be tested. A greater spillover of values-laden activity may be more likely to pervade the workplace, particularly in America, although elsewhere as well. The global profile of SRB has never been higher because of the U.N. Global Compact. Multistakeholder partnerships have evolved as a major new tool to tackle global problems such as access to life-saving drugs, the protection of human rights by the extractive industries, and eliminating sweatshop labor, which government clearly has not been able to resolve alone. At the same time, some of these partnerships would not have occurred were it not for the continued primacy that government plays in society. None of these partnerships would have occurred, nor would socially responsible businesses exist, without NGO pressure. SRB battles are fought in the streets and in the boardroom, with socially responsible investing providing the crucial bridge between the two. A key trend to watch in the future will be how the SRI field holds up through a potentially sustained global economic downturn, despite its phenomenal growth in recent years. The bottom line future of the SRB field lies in its intellectual development. More of the already impressive scholarly research needs to be produced and, just as important, be utilized far more widely in academia.

Socially responsible business itself, however, is not a trend. It is a permanent part of the global landscape.

2

SOCIAL RESPONSIBILITY AS A PROFESSIONAL VIRTUE

Law, Bourdieu, and Community

OSAGIE KINGSLEY OBASOGIE

While thinking about how to instill a consistent view of social responsibility in the "next generation," I immediately began to reflect upon my experiences with the law both as a student and as a professional advocate. Those outside of the legal profession may think that "social responsibility," however defined, is an inherent aspect of legal thought, training, and practice. As officers of the court, advocates for social change, and architects of rules and policies that structure many interactions and relationships, a rigorous and enduring commitment to community needs seems almost intuitive. However, despite noticeable instances of social consciousness, one can identify easily significant tensions that mitigate a more dynamic integration of social responsibility that prioritizes community needs as a meaningful professional virtue.

One such tension between legal discourse and social responsibility is that it exists primarily as a *formal* rather than a *substantive* pursuit. That is, the issue is not that contemporary notions of social responsibility within the legal field are wrong or non-existent, but that the way they are pursued is uniquely problematic. Legal minds tend to believe that within an adversarial system where individual interests are represented competently and compete in an impartial forum (e.g., the courts), the "winning" interest is seen formally as "right," and thus, *by definition*, in the best interest of society. From this perspective, zealous advocacy for "private" or individual interests ultimately achieves the "public" good.

This is empty formalism. The public/private divide, as an imposition on and not simply a reflection of the social world, acts as a principle means of vision and division within the legal field.[1] Within this field, responsibility to and respect for community values is often practiced as something anterior to the legal subject, presumably "safeguarded" in other legal arenas such as the legislative process or the democratic election of political representatives. What is recognized as a "public good" is often discernable from a lawyer's everyday "private" practice, which is presumed to be outside the scope of an overall ethos of advocating in a socially responsible manner. This chapter adopts sociological categories popularized by Pierre Bourdieu to explore the internal barriers that inhibit the "professionalization" of a more substantive ethos of social responsibility and seeks to understand how this problem is reflected in professions outside of the law.

The distinction between public and private spheres runs deep in American legal thought.[2] The myth that social, economic, and political activities can be bifurcated cleanly into mutually exclusive spheres inhibits an appreciation of the fluidity of social life and limits our imagination for remedies to social problems. As an analytic tool used to understand the weblike network of social relations that reflect and produce norms and behaviors within a specific segment of the population, Bourdieu's insights not only assist us in understanding the meaning of social responsibility to today's young professionals, but also creates a means to resituate a consistent vision of social responsibility in tomorrow's leaders. By using the public/private distinction as an entry point in which to understand how social responsibility operates within the legal field, this chapter looks at ethical rules as well as the professional externalities of the public/private divide to (1) explain the contemporary status of social responsibility within the legal field as an ideal anterior to their professional duties and (2) offer alternative approaches to rethinking and reconstituting professional fields whereby social responsibility can evolve into an embedded aspect of the professional identity of the "next generation."

Fields, Habitus, and Legal Ethics

Legal Thought as a Window into Social Relations

Throughout this chapter, the legal "field" is used as a site to discuss broader cultural and professional trends relating to social responsibility among today's professionals. This approach has not been chosen to privilege the legal experience over others, but to expose the interrelation between the legal field and larger social norms. Whether it is lawyers, investment bankers, government workers, or any other profession, the crux of one's professional identity invariably relies upon the perceived public or private character of the labor. The distinguishing characteristic often becomes whether or not your services are used for the promulgation of profit margins and/or individual wealth or for the betterment of society exclusive of individual financial reward.[3] While there are noticeable shades of gray, such intermediate organizational activity does not negate the perception or the reality that the public/private distinction is a central aspect of the social epistemology of labor.

It is difficult to discuss community issues, and furthermore social change, without appreciating the extent to which the law conditions, inhibits, and produces social and professional relations. Without question,

Legal discourse shapes our beliefs about the experiences and capacities of the human species, our conceptions of justice, freedom and fulfillment, and our visions of the future. It informs our beliefs about how people learn about and treat themselves and others, how we come to hold values, and how we might construct the institutions through which we govern ourselves. In these respects legal discourse resembles all other forms of systematized symbolic interaction. The peculiarity of legal discourse is that it tends to constrain the political imagination and to induce belief that our evolving social arrangements and institutions are just and rational, or at least inevitable, and therefore legitimate. The modus operandi of law as legitimating ideology is to make the historically contingent appear necessary. The function of legal discourse in our culture is to deny access to new modes of conceiving of democratic self governance, of our capacity for and the experience of freedom. Legal discourse inhibits the perception that we have it in our power to alter and abolish existing patterns of domination and denial of human potential. It is, in short, the vocation of legal thought to render radical, nonliberal visions of freedom literally inconceivable.[4]

Hence, the project is not to prioritize legal thought within broader discussions of social responsibility, but to understand how norms and beliefs within the legal field interact with other social and cultural fields to influence how social responsibility is shaped within the next generation of professionals. By using the public/private distinction to expose these tensions, one can begin to appreciate how this slice of thought and practice creates a baseline from which many professionals (mis)recognize their relationship with the ever growing needs of their surrounding communities.

Bourdieu's Theory of the Field

In its simplest form, Bourdieu's field theory describes the concurrent interdependence and relative autonomy of cultural and professional endeavors in relation to themselves and larger social, economic, and political structures. A central concept within this analysis is the idea that the social world exists as a network of relations in which each subset, or field, contains its own logic that is "specific and irreducible to those [logics] that regulate other fields,"[5] yet nonetheless shapes behaviors and interactions in the social world. Bourdieu notes, "for instance, the artistic field, or the religious field, or the economic field all follow specific logics: while the artistic field has constituted itself by rejecting or reversing the law of material profit, the economic field has emerged, historically, through the creation of a universe within which, as we commonly say, 'business is business,' where the enchanted relations of friendship and love are in principle excluded."[6] As a result, a field constitutes a miniature social world whereby participating individuals are simultaneously producers and consumers "caught in a complex web of social, political, economic, and cultural relations that they themselves have in part woven and continue to weave."[7]

As a formal matter, Bourdieu ascribes three steps to the analysis of a field.[8] First, one must examine the position of the field in relation to the field of power. Next, one should map out the struggle between agents who compete for the legitimate form of authority within the field. Last, Bourdieu asks that one investigate the extent to which agents have internalized the historical logics of the field (habitus) and the degree to which such internalizations have affected the trajectory of the field's materialization. Although the nature of this chapter does not permit a formal field analysis, aspects of this approach will be used to further our inquiries into the public/private distinction within the legal field and the projection of its logic onto the behaviors and desires of young professionals.

The Current State of Social Responsibility among Practicing Attorneys

One means to understand a professional's responsibility to community needs is to look at the ethical rules dictating her obligations. To the extent that Bourdieu compares a field to a game,[9] an investigation of professional ethics exposes the rules, beliefs, behaviors, and expectations of the individuals participating within that particular sphere of activity. While each profession undoubtedly has different approaches to social responsibility, the rules contextualizing the lawyer/client relationship exemplifies the public ramifications of the ethical fixation on ostensibly "private activities."

The American Bar Association[10] has adopted two standards of professional responsibility: The Model Rules of Professional Conduct ("The Model Rules") and The Model Code of Professional Responsibility ("The Code"). Although similar, the controlling ethical standard depends on which one is adopted by the relevant state bar association. It is important to understand that these ethical standards are not law in and of themselves. They merely explain the professional behavior that is expected by the state bar association and the courts. A lawyer acting outside of these rules risks professional sanctions, including disbarment. However, civil and personal liberties are not threatened by violating ethical standards, provided that the unethical conduct is not in furtherance of separate illegal acts.

What is apparent immediately is that neither the Model Rules nor the Code provides a meaningful discussion of a lawyer's obligation to social or community needs. Paragraph 11 of the preamble to the Model Rules broadly states that "the profession has a responsibility to assure that its regulations are conceived in the public interest," while the following paragraph states that "lawyers play a vital role in the preservation of society." Similarly, the preamble to the Code advocates aspirations for the preservation of society, while also stating that "a lawyer must with courage and foresight be able and ready to shape the body of the law to the ever-changing relationships of society."

In stark contrast, the ethical obligations surrounding the relationship between a lawyer and her individual client are discussed exhaustively. Western legal advocacy is grounded upon the sanctity of the lawyer/client relationship in that lawyers are expected to advocate their client's interest to the exclusion of any other. Unlike the amorphous references to social responsibility in the preambles, these are enumerated with particularity as distinct rules in which sanctions may be levied for their violation. For example, Rule 1.2(a) of the Model Rules states "a lawyer shall abide by a client's decisions concerning the objectives of representation, . . . and shall consult with the client as to the means by which they are to be pursued." While the Code does not reflect directly the sentiments expressed in the Model Rules, EC 7–7 does state affirmatively that "in certain areas of legal representation not affecting the merits of the case or substantially prejudicing the rights of the client, a lawyer is entitled to make decisions on his own. But otherwise the authority to make decisions is exclusively that of the client."

What are the implications? In essence, we have begun to see how the public/private distinction shapes the relationship between the legal professional, her client, and her responsibility to the public. By locating vague and non-binding "commitments" to social responsibility in the preambles of these ethical treatises while simultaneously predicating affirmative ethical obligations on the privacy[11] and primacy of the client-lawyer relationship, social responsibility functions as a pursuit tangential to the centrality and embeddedness of the client centered model of advocacy.

Although arguably an essential aspect of criminal proceedings,[12] the somewhat incidental nature of conscientious civil advocacy exemplifies how the public/private distinction adversely affects the sensibilities of social responsibility among all professionals. By categorizing social phenomena into either distinctively public or private realms, we reify the belief that private transactions are either positively or normatively anterior to social well-being. The private dispute between two individuals in court or the private transaction between two businessmen is not a public matter per se and thus notions of social responsibility somehow become moot. This "either or" rationale needs serious questioning as we pursue a more fluid conceptualization of what is public, what is private, and the professionals' duty to engage with community needs.

The Public/Private Distinction and Habitus

Bourdieu's notion of habitus plays an integral role within field theory. As a way to understand the autonomous yet binding effects of the intergenerational transmission of norms and behaviors, habitus becomes the means by which a "field analysis" accounts for the way in which "history turn[s] into nature."[13] It designates the extent to which certain logical and behavioral outcomes of a particular field develop absent the intent of any one particular agent, but in correlation with other structural desires. Bourdieu states that "in short, the habitus, the product of history, produces individual and collective practices, and hence history, in accordance with the schemes engendered by history."[14]

Understanding how the habitus of professional lawyering developed to exclude a substantive incorporation of social responsibility ultimately entails understanding the genealogy of the private/public distinction. Morton Horwitz states that the nineteenth-century emergence of the market as a central institution gave birth to the primacy of the public/private distinction in legal discourse. The nineteenth-century "obsession" with separating public and private law came from an effort to create a science that could distinguish between law and politics. As a crucial aspect of this new "science," private law was emphasized as a "neutral system for facilitating voluntary market transactions and vindicating injuries to private rights,"[15] in which the public or social consequences of such adjudications were deemed outside the scope of any legal remedy. This ethic of excluding public accountability from individual transactions "reflected the view that state regulation of private relations was a dangerous and unnatural public intrusion into a system based on private rights."[16] By defining the realm where state intrusion was preferable as public law (e.g., constitutional, criminal, and regulatory law) against the realm of private transactions (e.g., torts, contracts, and commercial law), the state, as an advocate of public/community needs, became incapable legally of regulating the externalities of many individual transactions.

To some, such a jurisprudential barrier on the state's reach is an appropriate check against the threat of totalitarian government. To others, the ideological promulgation of the "privacy" of certain transactions facilitates the economic correlation between profits and a deregulated business sector. Regardless, "the essence of the public/private distinction is the conviction that it is possible to conceive of social and economic life apart from government and law, indeed that it is impossible or dangerous to conceive of it any other way."[17] While this public/private habitus has a distinct genealogy within the legal field, its logic has broader implications on how individuals view themselves as socially responsible agents. As we observed in the Model Rules and the Code, the public/private habitus within the legal field intersects with larger economic influences (e.g., capitalism) to produce what can be called a market theory of social responsibility, where the interests that emerge victorious from private contests determine social goods and community needs. Furthermore, the distinct absence of a developed ethic of social responsibility creates a situation whereby it is not only permissible to advocate private interests to the exclusion of community needs, but one must do so or fear the professional sanctions and intrafield disrepute of not adhering to the ethical codes. Within this adversarial or market model of social consciousness, the private professional's only duty to social responsibility is to support her individual client's interest to the best of her ability, where the winning interest is formally viewed (and functions as) the best alternative for the community. In the next section, we will discuss approaches for the "next generation" in repositioning a robust conception of social responsibility as an embedded aspect of their professional endeavors.

Reshaping the Field: The Next Generation and an Alternative Habitus of Social Responsibility

Through the preceding analysis of the legal field and its relation to other professions, one can conclude that professionals face at least two distinct perspectives on public accountability, which includes: (1)

social responsibility does not necessarily inhere in being a lawyer or a professional per se, but in what *type* of professional one chooses to be and (2) social responsibility or general sensitivity to community needs is a choice *of some* rather than a expectation *of all*. For example, a lawyer on Wall Street may envision socially responsible advocacy as a professional obligation of public interest lawyers and thus not an affirmative obligation to his practice. Similarly, public interest lawyers may unduly shoulder the burden of advocating community needs without fully appreciating how the private sector can be a unique site for community involvement and improvement. What is needed is a different approach to social responsibility that locates its struggle within the individual regardless of professional affiliation with a for-profit or non-profit organization. This is not an indictment against the private sector for pursuing individual interest to the exclusion of communal needs, for it is not always self-evident that even self-proclaimed public interest advocates always have the public in mind. To the contrary, this is a criticism of how individuals on both sides of the public/private divide are trapped within a specific field of logic, have engendered a habitus of bifurcated professional responsibilities, and continue to reproduce this habitus through daily activities and choices that acculturate them to the idea that social responsibility and individual interests are mutually exclusive obligations that rest in one particular sector or another. What is needed is an understanding of how to recast collectively and relearn social responsibility as a personal commitment and not a product of one's *type* of work. This can create the foundations for a new professional habitus that transcends the public/private divide in reshaping the legal field as well as other professions.

Many considerations are important in promoting this new trajectory for professional habitus. While such projects are invariably complicated in that they conflict with many of the deepest beliefs held by individuals and organizations, it should begin with building seamless partnerships between what are currently recognized as public and private organizations to deemphasize any real or perceived distinctions that may inhibit future cooperation of the spheres. While many public/private partnerships currently exist, this model goes radically beyond mere philanthropy. There are considerable opportunities for advocating a more integrated approach that not only builds coalitions between public and private organizations, but also rethinks and reshapes the way business is done at the community if not the global level.

One way to rethink social responsibility along the public/private divide in a way that impacts tomorrow's leaders is to examine some of the opportunities available through professional schools. One promising example is the popularization of *pro bono* requirements as a condition of receiving one's professional degree. For example, in 1993, the faculty and administration at Columbia Law School adopted an initiative requiring all students to complete 40 hours of *pro bono* service before graduation.[18] Realizing that providing free legal services with public interest organizations can instill a sense of community awareness outside of traditional private practice, the law school embarked upon a program that aims to alter how students understand their professional relationship with their surrounding community. The mandatory *pro bono* service is not intended to initiate massive career changes within the student body, but rather to advocate through experience a notion of social responsibility that will hopefully follow them throughout their professional careers.

Other examples of public and private sector coalition building are the fellowships offered by private law firms to recent law school graduates who want to pursue public advocacy. In 1995, Kirkland and Ellis LLP made a $1 million gift to New York University School of Law and Columbia Law School to support one student from each school in one year of public service to the New York City community. These fellowships "are intended to put recent law school graduates to work meeting serious human needs in the New York City community, [in which the student] may create and fill a new position within an already-existing public service organization or pursue an independent public service project affiliated with a sponsoring organization."[19] Similarly, the law firm of Skadden, Arps, Slate, Meager, and Flom LLP has established The Skadden Foundation which awards thirty fellowships to recent law school graduates who create their own projects in "provid[ing] legal services to the poor, elderly, homeless and disabled, as well as those deprived of their human or civil rights. In recent years, Fellows have also worked on issues concerning economic development and community renewal."[20]

These examples demonstrate how innovative strategies of coalition building can provide opportunities and resources to young professionals in rethinking their identity as well as their subsequent commitment to community needs. By having a growing number of private firms support public deeds, even those individuals who do not participate directly can be inspired by the firms' commitment to community goals outside of individual profit margins. Similarly, Columbia's mandatory *pro bono* requirement ensures that every student has a professional experience that emphasizes community values as opposed to personal compensation.

While significant, these examples are not unproblematic. By having private organizations advocate *pro bono* work, it may reaffirm and reconstitute the preexisting habitus within the field that the public/private divide is meaningful, thereby further entrenching the belief that community minded lawyering is and should be external to private obligations. While not a complete epistemological overlap, these examples provide an important first step in promoting integrated contact between the spheres.

In order to transcend fully this dilemma, such partnerships must be expanded throughout all social sectors so as to redefine the relationship between private professionals and community needs. When coalition models such as those exhibited by Kirkland and Ellis, Skadden, Arps, and Columbia Law School become mainstream mechanisms of doing business and educating young professionals, the next generation cannot help but to have a more symbiotic understanding of social responsibility that inheres within their own professional sensibilities rather than their job descriptions. Furthermore, ethical regulations such as the Model Rules and the Code should be revised to promote community minded lawyering as an affirmative duty of each lawyer in addition to a client's immediate interests.

Various incentives can be used to establish and expand the partnerships of traditionally public and private organizations. David Maurrasse has written extensively on partnerships between academic institutions and community organizations, arguing that

> At all levels of higher education, . . . community partnerships make sense to varying degrees for colleges and universities, in both academic and economic dimensions of their missions. Mutual interests between local communities and institutions of higher education do exist, and they seem to become more apparent through lengthy relationship building processes.[21]

In a sense, the incentive for academic institutions is already there. By simply reaching out to their surrounding communities, Maurrasse persuasively argues that partnerships benefit education as much as the community. One challenge is to expose these connections and mutual interests through continued scholarly works such as Maurrasse's and through grassroots coalition building as pursued by organizations such as the Center for Innovation in Social Responsibility (CISR).[22]

In the realm of business, the ultimate challenge involves demonstrating how the elimination of the public/private divide is not only morally or socially desirable, but also advantageous to individual business interests. Certain incentives can be incorporated, such as tax credits or other financial breaks for private firms that foster significant relationships with established community organizations. Such incentives can encourage private organizations to think outside of its field of logic to explore the advantages of partnering with and investing in their surrounding communities. This does not simply mean offering free professional services or making tax deductible contributions, but substantively incorporating community interests into daily business practices. Some examples follow.

- In the legal field, this may include counseling clients not only on the individual consequences of civil actions or corporate transactions, but also advising on the potentially harmful externalities endured by the community, ways to avoid them, as well as ways to use individual litigation to benefit the community.
- Within investment banking, it may involve advising clients not only to invest in high return markets, but also to diversify their practices by investing in community organizations and small businesses.
- Within consulting, this may include advising clients on how to simultaneously attain individual goals and community needs by formulating strategies that carefully balance both pursuits.

In essence, the same imagination used to create profits can be incentivized to diminish the public/private divide, create community strength, and provide a basis for a generation of leaders whose sense of social responsibility will create and be driven by an evolving habitus that embraces the ethics of communal responsibility and public accountability.

3

ENVIRONMENTAL RESULTS

Corporations, Financial Markets, and Environmental Sustainability

FRANK DIXON

Environmental sustainability looms as one of the greatest challenges ever faced by business. Financial impacts on companies are growing as customers, regulators, investors, and other stakeholders continue to press for improvements in corporate environmental performance and movement toward sustainability.[1] This drives increasing demand from the financial community for high-quality analysis of corporate environmental performance. The sophistication of analysis has increased greatly over the past five years; however, limited data availability poses ongoing challenges for capital markets, business, and other interested parties, such as nongovernmental organizations (NGOs).

As environmental conditions continue to decline globally, and calls for action to address the situation increase, the need grows for performance data at the macro- and microlevels. The availability of transparent, high-quality data spurs competition and performance improvement. At the macrolevel, data quality varies greatly by region. At the microlevel, corporate environmental performance data are often unavailable, inconsistent, lagged, inaccurate, unverified, and biased. This lack of high-quality data clouds relative corporate environmental performance, reduces the efficiency of markets, and presents a significant barrier to meeting the sustainability challenge.

This chapter discusses what drives growing financial community interest in corporate environmental performance, methods of measuring such performance, and future measurement challenges. The

EcoValue'21™ model, developed by Innovest Strategic Value Advisors, is presented to illustrate one method of addressing data challenges and to show how environmental performance ratings can be used to increase investor returns.

Overall, the chapter argues that the financial relevance of corporate environmental performance is increasing, and this will drive expanded incorporation of environmental analysis into investment decisions. Ultimately, ongoing improvements in corporate environmental performance data will be needed to minimize investor risk and maximize financial returns.

Financial Community Interest in Corporate Environmental Performance

The corporate sector has a large impact on the environment through waste emissions to land, air, and water resulting from production, use, and disposal of goods and services. This impact contributes to the ongoing decline in global environmental quality. Deteriorating environmental conditions translate into financial pressures on companies through increasing regulations; growing demand from consumers for environmentally responsible products, services, and corporate policies; political pressures; rapidly expanding information transparency, largely through the Internet; growing concern among the general public about the state of the environment; increasing investor awareness of the financial benefits of improving corporate environmental performance; and growing competition among firms to improve their pollution control and natural resource management results. As environmental pressures continue to increase, companies that improve environmental performance more than their peers are likely to achieve superior financial returns and competitive positioning over the mid to long term. In addition, corporate environmental leaders frequently report achieving enhanced profitability in the short term.

In spite of this growing financial relevance, mainstream investors traditionally have not incorporated environmental analysis into investment decisions. The financial community can thus be segregated into two groups: mainstream investors and those who are socially responsible (i.e., basing investments on environmental, social, and financial considerations). Traditionally, mainstream investors (representing about 85 percent of invested assets in the United States) considered environmental issues only to a limited degree. The environment was seen as a potential liability (e.g., Superfund sites), risk (e.g., catastrophic event), and/or cost item (e.g., regulatory compliance). It was not seen traditionally as a source of competitive advantage or investment outperformance. The concept of fiduciary responsibility has limited use of environmental analysis in the investment process. This concept holds that the duty to maximize investor returns precludes consideration of issues that do not seem to be relevant financially to the company, such as the longer term impacts of pollution on the environment and society.

More recently, mainstream investors, such as Dreyfus and Mellon Capital Management, have been using relative corporate environmental performance to differentiate companies and increase investment return. Several factors drive growing financial community interest in corporate environmental performance. First, most studies of links between environmental and financial performance find positive correlations. Second, a reasonable theory exists for explaining correlations and postulating causation—environmental performance is a strong proxy for management quality. Third, socially responsible investment funds (which include environmentally screened funds) frequently outperform nonscreened funds. Fourth, growing pressure for corporations to assume fuller responsibility for their environmental and social impacts increases investor risk exposure. And, finally, recent regulatory requirements and evolving legal views encourage or mandate increased investor focus on corporate environmental performance.

Research Findings

Since 1990, most studies of links between corporate environmental and financial performance found positive correlations.[2] A U.S. Environmental Protection Agency study (2000) found, "A significant body of academic research relates measures of corporate environmental performance to measures of financial performance. The most striking aspect of this research is that most of it shows a moderate positive relationship between the two kinds of performance—regardless of the variables used to represent each kind of performance, the technique used to analyze the relationship, or the date of the study. In fact, the empirical evidence is of sufficient consistency and scale to embolden some to argue that a positive relationship between environmental and financial performance is without doubt."

A recent review (Cram and Koehler, 2001) of more than forty studies in this area found, "The 1990's has seen an expanding series of studies probing at the association between a firm's environmental and financial performance with the general conclusion that it is statistically significant." Another study by Bank Sarasin (Butz and Plattner, 1999) concluded, "there is definitely a statistically significant positive correlation between environmental performance and the financial return on equities in sectors where environmental performance is relevant in the public perception."

Positive correlations are also often found in the broader socially responsible investing category, which analyzes social (e.g., labor, supply chain, product safety, international, community development, etc.) and environmental metrics. For instance, Pava and Krausz (1995) examined twenty-one empirical studies and found that twelve had positive correlations, eight had no statistically significant correlation, and only one had a negative correlation.

The EPA and Cram and Koehler studies point out various gaps and errors in some of the previous research that could produce misleading results. Potential flaws in some of the studies include poor data quality, small sample size, short time frame, inadequate control of nonenvironmental factors influencing financial performance, inappropriate cross-sectoral comparisons, emphasis on backward-looking data, failure to establish causation, vulnerability to greenwashing,[3] difficulty in assessing impacts on human health and the environment, and inconsistent definitions of environmental performance. To illustrate the complexity of definition problems, Cram and Koehler note that performance based on emissions will improve if a company divests itself of a polluting facility. But if the company continues to buy materials from the same facility, its overall environmental performance may not actually improve.

The Cram and Koehler draft concludes that study flaws "raise considerable doubt on the findings described in the literature thus far" and that this literature "offers no conclusive guidance on managerial and investor decision-making with respect to firm environmental performance." However, the implication that positive correlations found in the bulk of previous research may not be valid due to study flaws is probably too aggressive for several reasons. First, most of the alleged flaws have about equal probabilities of producing false negative and positive correlations. In other words, most of the potential flaws do not bias the studies toward finding positive correlations. The fact that positive correlations nevertheless are found consistently indicates that the overall findings are probably valid.

Second, Cram and Koehler argue that, as more sophisticated modeling techniques are employed to overcome earlier flaws, positive correlations are still found. Third, measuring highly complex environmental interactions with frequently poor data sometimes requires simplifying of assumptions and use of suboptimal data sets. These approaches are open to challenge, but without them, research in this area could hardly be done. Fourth, failure to show causation does not invalidate the findings because investors frequently make investment decisions based on factors, such as earnings, that are known to be correlated with but may not be causally linked, to stock price. (In the strictest sense, it is impossible to prove direct causation between stock price and anything since stock price is a collective market opinion.)

Fifth, the authors imply that investors would use analysis of corporate environmental performance exclusively to choose stocks. Except for eco-enhanced index strategies, this rarely occurs. Environmental analysis typically is used in combination with traditional financial analysis to identify well-managed companies and stock market outperformance potential (discussed below). And, finally, Cram and Koehler do not address adequately the fact that there is a logical and intuitively obvious explanation for the existence of positive correlations—the proxy value for management quality.

More research is needed in this area to test the existence of positive correlations between environmental and financial performance. Cram and Koehler's implication that the existing research is flawed, and investors cannot rely upon it, is probably overly critical. However, the authors add significant value by pointing out methodological weaknesses and suggesting "future directions for this body of research."

Management Quality and Other Explanatory Factors

Causation is notoriously difficult to prove because so many factors influence financial performance. As a result, studies often focus on explaining correlations rather than attempting to prove causation. Several of the studies using historical data to identify correlations between environmental and financial performance cite management quality as a primary explanation. Future-oriented assessments of corporate environmental performance, such as those done by Innovest, find positive correlations more frequently and attribute the findings largely to management quality. This factor probably has a greater influence on financial performance than any other. Management quality influences all aspects of business performance, largely determining success in key functional areas such as product development, marketing, and production. One could say that most factors enabling firms to outperform peers, such as lower costs or strong patent protection, originate from superior management.

Nearly every financial analyst would agree that management quality is one of the primary determinates of financial performance. However, very few have an objective way of measuring management quality. Assessments are usually subjective, based on opinion. Management quality is difficult to quantify because it involves assessing intangible factors such as the intelligence and business savvy of corporate leaders. Assessing management quality can be done by using proxies—for example, by measuring some aspect of management performance, rather than trying to measure management quality directly. This, in effect, is done by analyzing earnings and other financial measures. However, there are so many other internal and external influences that the pure assessment of management quality is clouded. A clearer assessment can be made by narrowing the focus to one issue. In other words, test how well management performs in one business area, preferably a highly complex area. Success here implies that management will deal effectively with less complex business issues and, therefore, will produce superior returns.

It turns out that the environment is one of the most complex challenges facing management, especially in resource-intensive sectors, where there is a high degree of technical, regulatory, and market uncertainty. There are many internal and external stakeholders to deal with, requiring sophisticated communication skills. There are many complex issues to address, such as global warming. And there are many nontraditional, often nonfinancial metrics to track. It is implied that companies dealing well with this high level of complexity have the sophistication to succeed in other parts of the business. The relationship between good environmental management and good general management may explain why companies recognized as environmental leaders frequently earn superior financial and stock market returns.

Another factor explaining correlations between environmental and financial performance is the direct impact improved environmental performance can have on profitability. Specifically, improving environmental performance can lower risk exposure and costs and increase revenues. Improving performance can lower risk exposure in many areas, including damage to corporate image and reputation, loss of market share, vulnerability to increasing regulations, product obsolescence, impairment of property values, and delay or cancellation of mergers and acquisitions. On the upside, reported financial benefits of improved environmental performance include reduced materials, energy, and waste disposal costs; enhanced product quality, market image, and market share; lower regulatory, insurance, and financing costs; enhanced innovation capacity; improved stakeholder relations; and enhanced employee morale and productivity. For example, 3M claims to have saved $810 million between 1975 and 1997 through pollution prevention initiatives (3M, 1998).

Companies improve environmental performance when the perceived benefits of doing so exceed the costs. However, benefits can be intangible, longer term, and sometimes simply difficult to quantify. As a result, it may be hard to financially justify investments focused on improving environmental performance. Our research suggests that leading companies tend to have greater ability to deal with intangibles, such as future market perceptions or the indirect financial impacts of pollution. At times, these firms will make marginal improvements in environmental performance that may not make sense on a strict internal rate of return basis. They perceive financial bene-fits that less sophisticated companies may not be able to see. The complexity of environmental decision making further indicates why environmental performance can be used to differentiate management quality and stock market potential.

Some studies suggest that positive correlation may also occur be-cause more profitable companies may be able to spend more on the environment. Across the spectrum of companies, it is likely that all three explanations are valid—proxy value for management quality, direct impacts on profitability, and superior profits driving superior environmental performance. More research is needed to determine the relative importance of each factor in producing a positive correla-tion between environmental and financial performance.

Fund Performance

Traditionally, most investment advisors have believed that screening investments for environmental, social, or any other so-called nonfi-nancial criteria reduced financial returns, even though most studies have shown the opposite. Inappropriate fund comparisons have con-tributed to the idea that socially responsible investment funds under-perform. For example, some studies inappropriately have grouped different types of funds (value, growth, etc.) together and compared them to other fund classes. However, socially responsible investing is a discipline that can be applied to all fund classes; it is not a separate fund class.

Earlier approaches that used negative environmental and social screening exclusively did underperform the market at times.[4] Newer fund strategies using best-in-class approaches that maintain diversity and shift investments toward presumably better managed companies frequently have outperformed nonscreened (mainstream) funds. More recently, both negatively screened and best-in-class (or posi-tively screened) funds often have matched or exceeded the perfor-mance of mainstream funds. For example, fourteen of the sixteen environmentally and socially screened funds with over $100 million in assets received top scores from rating services Morningstar and

Lipper Analytical Services in 2000. Overall, 65 percent of the funds with a greater than three-year performance record received top scores (Social Investment Forum, 2001).

The availability of better information on environmentally and socially screened fund performance and findings from the many studies noted above is causing a growing belief in the financial community that environmental and social screening does not lower returns and, in many cases, may enhance them. This partly explains the rapid growth of these funds in North America, Europe, and Japan over the past five years. At the end of 1999, environmentally and socially screened investments represented over $2 trillion in U.S. assets (Social Investment Forum, 1999).

The Evolving Role of Corporations in Society

As environmental conditions continue to decline, companies may be called on to take fuller responsibility for their negative environmental impacts and to adopt a systems view of the environment. As firms are held responsible for a wider range of impacts, investor risk exposure likely will increase. Before the Industrial Revolution, society's impact on the environment was insignificant in relation to the ability of the environment to absorb the impact. Driven largely by the use of fossil and nuclear energy, human impacts are now significant and may be approaching the point of overwhelming the environment's ability to regenerate itself. All aspects of Earth and its atmosphere are one interconnected system. No part operates in isolation. Traditionally, the total Earth system was too complex to study as a whole. Through reductionism, the parts were studied in-depth. However, the overall system and relationships between its parts were not studied nearly as well. As a result, solutions to problems in one area became problems in another, as in fossil fuel combustion causing global warming.

Economic and commercial systems developed when human impacts on the environment were relatively small and did not hold companies fully accountable for the harm they inflicted on the environment. For example, these systems considered clean air and water to be free goods because they were so plentiful. As a result, companies were not charged the full cost of consuming these and other resources. Their focus was only on the efficient production of goods and services.

Now, as the negative environmental impacts of companies have become more obvious, these costs, which have largely been externalized onto society, are being internalized through increasing regulations, customer demands, taxes, and other mechanisms. To an increasing degree, companies are being called on to expand their operating focus to include being a responsible corporate citizen and minimizing their negative environmental and social impacts. Companies failing to move in this direction likely will face growing financial risks and penalties directly from government imposed regulations and indirectly from customers and capital markets.

Regulatory and Legal Issues

Growing financial market interest in corporate environmental performance is being driven by regulatory requirements and evolving legal views on the fiduciary responsibilities of fund advisors. For example, the U.K. government implemented legislation in July 2000 that requires pension funds to disclose their methods of screening investments for environmental, social, and ethical factors. As a result, twenty-two of the twenty-five largest pension funds in the United Kingdom have adopted such screening methods.

In the legal area, a significant barrier to the use of environmental and social screening has been the belief that directors of pension and other funds have a fiduciary responsibility to maximize returns, which precludes them from considering so-called nonfinancial factors, such as environmental and social performance. This view is changing as studies by organizations such as the law firm of Baker & McKenzie (Gibson, Levitt and Cargo, 2000) find that fiduciaries may consider environmental and social issues when making investment decisions, provided there is reasonable due diligence.[5] Beyond allowing environmental and social screening, other studies find that, in some cases, the duty to monitor (Koppes and Reilly, 1995) and the duty of obligation (Cogan, 2000; McKeown, 1997; Solomon and

Coe, 1997) place fiduciaries under a legal requirement to consider environmental and social issues.

Measuring Corporate Environmental Performance

How do the capital markets identify superior environmental performance? Corporate environmental performance remains hard to measure, yet, new quantitative analytic tools are being developed. For example, Innovest's EcoValue'21™ model mitigates data problems and provides a relevant and objective measurement tool for the financial community. This section discusses the current state of corporate environmental performance data, measurement options and complexity, analytic methods, measurement results, and application by the financial community.

Data Quality

Standardized public financial reporting has been required in industrialized nations for many years. As a result, it is relatively easy for stakeholders to compare firms on many financial metrics. The requirement for standardized public reporting is not nearly as well developed in the environmental area. While U.S. global leadership has diminished markedly in recent years, the U.S. government remains the world leader in providing publicly available data that permit analysis of corporate environmental performance.

The U.S. Environmental Protection Agency (EPA) provides several publicly available databases,[6] including:

- Toxic Release Inventory (TRI; provides data on releases and transfers of more than six hundred toxic chemicals from manufacturing facilities)
- Emergency Response Notification System (ERNS; tracks spills and releases of toxic substances)
- Accidental Release Information Program (updates the ERNS database)
- Water Permit Compliance System (tracks permit violations and penalties assessed under the Clean Water Act)

- Resource Conservation and Recovery Act Information System (tracks handlers of hazardous waste under the RCRA)
- RCRA Biennial Reporting System (tracks the generation and shipment of hazardous waste)
- EPA Legal Action Data (tracks civil cases filed on behalf of the EPA)
- Comprehensive Environmental Response, Compensation, and Liability Act (CERCLA) Information System (tracks hazardous waste sites under the Superfund Program)

While this information facilitates corporate environmental performance measurement, many improvements still could be made. For example, the TRI tracks emissions from domestic manufacturing facilities; however, because data on the environmental impacts of non-manufacturing and international operations usually are not available, it's difficult to compare companies with significant activities in these areas. Also, there is often a long lag time before data are made public. In addition, information is reported at the facility level, and tagging methods often make it difficult to attribute the data correctly to the ultimate parent company. Finally, data often are uploaded by different states and regional EPA offices, making their quality uneven. Through various initiatives, the EPA is attempting to remedy some of these issues.

Some European governments, such as those in the United Kingdom and Sweden, require limited disclosure of corporate environmental performance data. However, varying disclosure requirements in Europe make it difficult to compare companies, especially those with operations in many countries. The European Union is working to standardize disclosure requirements, so it is likely that higher quality government-supplied data will be available in Europe over the next few years. Beyond government databases, various types of corporate environmental performance data are available from NGOs and watchdog groups.

While government-supplied data are useful, especially in the United States, the most complete source of corporate environmental performance data is usually the companies themselves. Government-supplied data in Europe are sparse compared with the United States.

However, European companies generally provide higher quality data on corporate environmental performance (with many exceptions in North America and Japan). Companies in Europe tend to report more consistent quantified data on environmental impacts. This type of information is more useful to those assessing relative performance than the anecdotal information usually provided by less proactive firms. The quality and quantity of data provided by European firms often more than compensates for the lack of government-supplied data in Europe.

However, corporate self-initiative data not reported under mandatory disclosure schemes remain open to reliability questions. To reduce the perception that company-supplied data are biased, many European firms are seeking third-party certification of their environmental reports. While third-party verification does not eliminate bias potential, since companies still chose which data to report, it is a first step toward providing investors with more reliable data. To improve data quality further, several firms in Europe and North America are beginning to report under standardized environmental and social reporting schemes, such as the Global Reporting Initiative. Expanded use of programs like these has significant potential to facilitate corporate measurement of environmental performance. However, as long as the programs remain voluntary, their usefulness will be limited.

In the United States, accounting rules for contingent liabilities can result in significant underreporting of environmental liabilities. For example, Financial Accounting Standards Board Statement No. 5 states that contingent liabilities, such as environmental remediation liabilities, shall only be accrued if they are probable and can be estimated reasonably. If the estimated cost is within a range, only the minimum cost shall be accrued. Disclosure is only required if a claim has been made, or it is probable one will be made. As a result, financial statements may understate significantly environmental liabilities. This could have a growing negative impact on investors as environmental pressures on companies increase.

A recent study of thirteen pulp and paper companies (Repetto and Austin, 2000) found that each company could expect negative financial impacts from environmental issues of at least five percent of total shareholder value (more than 10 percent for some companies) and that these highly probable impacts were not disclosed in financial statements. Several parties, including the investment firm Calvert Group, have asked the U.S. Securities and Exchange Commission (SEC) to increase investor protection by expanding current disclosure requirements. The SEC has explored the issue, but has not acted yet. Mandatory disclosure of corporate environmental performance data probably holds the greatest potential for facilitating measurement and prompting competition among firms to improve performance.

Measurement Issues and Complexity

Corporate environmental performance assessments can be done in many ways. Options include absolute versus best-in-class ratings, one versus many scores, and historical versus forward-looking analysis. Absolute ratings potentially describe a company's ultimate environmental impact more accurately and facilitate cross-sector comparisons. However, investors primarily use corporate environmental performance analysis to choose among companies within sectors, so a best-in-class approach is generally most effective. Condensing many metrics into one score provides less information than several separate scores. However, having a bottom-line score helps investors chose among companies, so a single-score approach remains effective. Historical analysis provides a more accurate assessment of a company's actual environmental impact. However, investors are interested in future performance, so a forward-looking analysis is often more appropriate, although forecasting future results is much more difficult than reporting on past performance.

Beyond numerous assessment options, difficulty in quantifying corporate environmental impacts further complicates performance measurement. As companies are held responsible for a wider range of environmental impacts, minimizing investor risk will require ongoing improvements in corporate impact data. Yet, quantifying corporate impacts is difficult because Earth's ecosystem is multifaceted and highly complex. The sinks into which companies emit waste (i.e., atmosphere, water bodies, land masses) are so large that there are often long feedback loops before impacts can be identified. It is difficult to quantify a firm's impact on the environment because of these long feedback loops and because impacts can take many forms (e.g., human health, ecosystem damage, biodiversity loss, etc.). In addition, it is often difficult to pinpoint a firm's contribution to a specific impact.

By using proxies and impact indicators, assessing environmental impact can be simplified, assuming the data are made available. To illustrate, many companies, mostly in Europe, are reporting impacts under standard categories, such as global warming, ozone depletion, acidifying emissions, smog-forming emissions, eutrophication, toxic wastes, water use, energy use, and heavy metals. This facilitates cross-company comparisons and helps to minimize investor risk exposure.

Analyzing Corporate Environmental Performance

Throughout the industrialized world, a mix of nonprofit and for-profit organizations analyzes corporate environmental performance and provides this information to investors and other stakeholders. For the most part, this analysis involves gathering data through questionnaires, then summarizing anecdotal and quantitative data (when available). Some firms, such as Kinder Lydenberg and Domini, assign ratings in various environmental and social categories, but most organizations are in the business of providing summarized data to investors, who then do the analysis on their own. Fewer firms provide financially oriented analysis of corporate environmental performance data.

The EcoValue'21™ model, developed by Innovest Strategic Value Advisors, uses a multifactored approach to overcome data problems and assess corporate environmental performance more accurately. Using one or only a few data points to assess performance makes the analysis vulnerable to "outliers" and other data weaknesses, potentially providing misleading results, because so many factors influence overall environmental performance. A multifactored analysis minimizes the impact of faulty data since, even if a few data points are inaccurate, companies usually will be placed in nearly the same relative order based on overall averages.

To assess corporate environmental performance, one must first define it; however, with many interpretations available, there is no one "correct" definition. Definitions vary based on the goals of the user. An investor seeking to gauge the financial impact of corporate environmental performance likely would want to assess the financially relevant aspects of a company. These include risk exposure, upside potential (engagement in environmentally related business opportunities), and overall management of upside and downside environmental issues. The EcoValue'21™ model analyzes about sixty metrics grouped into these three categories. While the model was developed for investors focused on financial performance, its comprehensive nature allows it to be used by other stakeholders who are purely interested in environmental performance.

Metrics and weightings for the EcoValue'21™ model were selected using criteria that included the quality of available data (with preference given to quantitative, third-party verified data), business judgment about the relative importance of the metric to overall corporate environmental performance and, most important, correlations with stock returns, since the model was being used to project this. The model was developed with strategic partners, including PriceWaterhouseCoopers and Morgan Stanley. To guide selection of metrics and determination of metric weights, regression analysis was done to analyze correlations between many environmental metrics and stock returns for 350 S&P 500 companies over a five-year period.

In the risk area, the model analyzes such factors as site liabilities, hazardous waste generation, toxic emissions, compliance violations, spills and releases, and other indicators of environmental burden, such as those frequently published by European firms (as noted above). In addition, energy and resource use efficiency is assessed, along with market and regulatory risk exposure. Beyond these general categories, sector-specific metrics are analyzed based on the relevant risk factors for each sector. Examples include fuel mix in the electric utility sector, exposure to EPA's Cluster Rule in the pulp and paper sector, and fuel efficiency in the automotive sector. A key element of the analysis is adjusting for risk exposure among companies in the same sector due to such factors as product mix and geographic location. In addition, the model analyzes performance over time as well as static risk indicators. Especially in terms of risk, preference is given to quantitative data or, when such data are not available, qualitative assessments.

In the opportunity area, the model analyzes capacity to develop environmentally favorable products and services, market positioning to sell them effectively, and actual involvement in marketing them. Capacity indicators include resources devoted to this area, research and development focus, and strategic planning procedures. Market positioning indicators include geographic regions served, demographics of customer base, and vulnerability to substitution. Involvement indicators include assessing the extent to which companies are developing and/or marketing environmentally favorable products and service.

The EcoValue'21™ model is strongly future-oriented. As a result, factors such as management of environmental issues and strategic positioning are weighted more heavily. Beyond risk assessment, quantitative assessments of historic and current environmental performance are used to authenticate stated commitments to improving corporate environmental performance; in other words, to verify that the company is "walking its talk" and to avoid being "greenwashed."

In terms of management, the model analyzes many planning, environmental management systems (EMS), and governance metrics. Planning indicators include the extent to which environmental issues are incorporated into the overall business strategy. This includes an assessment of the degree to which the environment is being used to build competitive advantage rather than being used only for public relations purposes. EMS indicators include the quality of the environmental policy; use of life-cycle analysis to assess impacts; evaluation of eco-efficiency initiatives; EMS quality, including the use of third-party certification schemes such as ISO 14001; performance monitoring and accounting systems; training procedures; supplier screening and engagement programs; quality of public reporting; auditing procedures; and participation in voluntary programs and product labeling schemes. Governance indicators include board involvement, management structure, compensation programs, and more subjective indicators such as company culture and senior management commitment.

Implementing the EcoValue'21™ process involves first assessing the key upside and downside environmental issues in each sector and analyzing the strategies of sector leaders. This information is used to build a template against which the sector is analyzed. Then information is gathered from such sources as government databases, NGOs, periodical and web searches, financial community reports, and company information, including annual reports, 10Ks, 10Qs, environmental and sustainability reports, web sites and any other available publications. Following this, company executives (often vice presidents of environment or health and safety) are interviewed to complete the data-gathering process.

Once data are gathered for each of the roughly sixty Eco-Value'21™ metrics, weightings are assigned as described above. These weighted scores are added to produce bottom-line numeric scores for each company in a given sector. Then best-in-class letter scores, ranging from AAA to CCC, are assigned to project relative stock market performance. The following box provides the rationale for the rating of one company, FPL Group.

FPL Group

FPL Group, the parent of Florida Power & Light, received an AAA EcoValue'21™ rating in the U.S. electric utility sector. The rating reflects FPL's moderate risk level, excellent risk management, and sector-leading development of environmentally favorable businesses. With a diversified fuel mix, the company has lower risk exposure than those relying more heavily on coal or nuclear. Proactive risk management includes extensive training and performance measurement, linking compensation to environmental performance, and implementing a leading environmental management system. Aggressive efforts to improve eco-efficiency include improving power plant efficiency, extensive recycling, and replacing toxic materials with lower impact substitutes. FPL is also one of the largest developers of wind power in the United States.

Measurement Results

The EcoValue'21™ model was designed to estimate stock market potential over the mid- to longer term. The model is not intended to forecast short-term stock market potential; nevertheless, it has been successful in doing so. In every high-environmental-impact sector and nearly every other sector, the average total stock market return of companies with above-average EcoValue'21™ ratings exceeded the average return of bottom-half companies by three hundred to three thousand basis points per year. (Established in 1996, Innovest has rated more than one thousand two hundred mostly large-cap companies in North America, Europe, and Asia.) Table 3.1 shows top-half/bottom-half differentials in a few sectors.[7]

Table 3.1   EcoValue'21™ Performance

Sector	Time Period	Top-Half/Bottom-Half Differential (basis points)
Electric utilities (U.S.)	8/98–7/01	4,000
Automobiles (global)	3/99–3/01	2,300
Mining (global)	2/98–2/01	2,200
Food (global)	9/97–9/00	3,500
Steel (global)	8/97–8/00	2,700

A study by QED International Associates (Blank and Carty, 2001) further illustrates how environmental ratings can be used to enhance investor returns. In the study, three different tests of EcoValue'21™ were conducted. In the first test, the stock market returns of two equally weighted portfolios were compared, top-rated companies (AAA and AA—27 percent of the rated universe) versus the universe of companies rated by Innovest for the years 1997 to 2000. Over the entire period, the top-rated companies returned 12.4 percent annually, compared with 8.9 percent for the entire universe of rated stocks. The top-rated portfolio also had lower volatility than the total universe. (More detailed results and a fuller explanation of the study are available at www.innovestgroup.com.)

Figure 3.1 shows that $10,000 invested in the Innovest-ranked universe would have grown to $14,037 over four years, compared with $15,946 for the top-ranked companies.

To neutralize the effect of varying sector weights, which may have affected results in the first test, a second test was conducted. In this case, a portfolio was constructed that had the same risk profile as the S&P 500, but favored stocks that were rated highly by Innovest, subject to a 50-basis point tracking error. This portfolio was compared to the S&P 500. Figure 3.2 shows that the Innovest-enhanced portfolio grew from $10,000 to $21,980, compared with $18,782 for the S&P 500 over the years 1997 to 2000. The enhanced portfolio also displayed lower volatility than the S&P 500 over the four-year period. QED estimates that roughly half of the widening performance differential in 2000 is due to the downturn in Internet-related stocks.

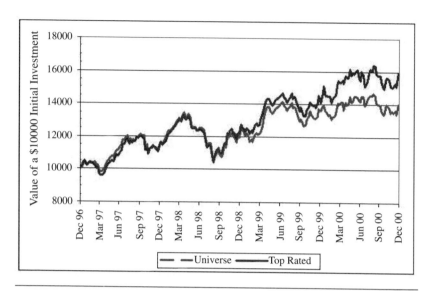

Figure 3.1 Growth of a $10,000 Investment of Top-rated Stocks Compared with the Total Universe
Source: Innovest and QED International Associates, Inc.

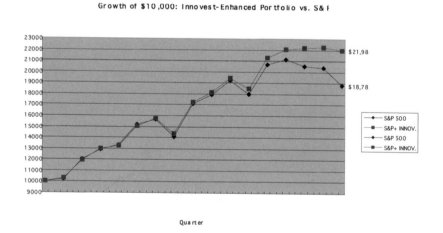

Growth of $10,000: Innovest-Enhanced Portfolio vs. S&P

Figure 3.2 Growth of $10,000 in the Value of Portfolios Tilted to Top-rated Stocks Compared with S&P 500
Source: Innovest and QED International Associates, Inc.

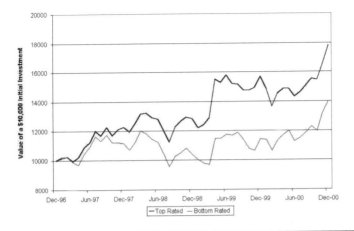

Figure 3.3 A Comparison of the Growth of a $10,000 Investment in Top- and Bottom-rated Stocks in Environmentally Intense Industry Groups
Source: Innovest and QED International Associates, Inc.

The third test of the EcoValue'21™ model compares top-rated companies (AAA and AA) with bottom-rated companies (B and CCC) in the most environmentally sensitive sectors (chemicals, electric utilities, forest products, mining, petroleum, and steel) over the four-year period from 1997 to 2000. Figure 3.3 shows that the portfolio of top-ranked stocks grew to $17,844 in four years, compared with $14,043 for the bottom-ranked stocks. Over the entire period, the top-rated companies returned 18 percent annually compared to10.2 percent for the bottom-rated companies.

The primary reason for the short-term outperformance of environmental leaders found in Innovest's sector analyses and the QED study is most likely that the EcoValue'21™ ratings are gauging management quality accurately. In effect, the ratings assess management's ability to deal with complexity, address forces acting on the company, and modify strategies accordingly. As environmental pressures on firms continue to increase, it is likely that stock market performance differentials between environmental leaders and laggards also will grow. As a result, the importance of incorporating corporate environmental performance analysis into investment decisions most likely will increase over time.

Application by the Financial Community

Many pension funds, asset managers, and other financial sector organizations use research on corporate environmental performance to help guide equity investments. The large majority of these investments are made through traditional negative screening approaches. However, a growing number of mainstream financial firms use relative environmental performance under a best-in-class, or positive screening, approach. For example, firms including ABN-AMRO, Bank Sarasin, Cambridge Associates, Neuberger Berman, Rockefeller & Co., Schroders, Société Generale, T. Rowe Price, and Zurich Scudder purchase environmental and social research and advisory services from Innovest. Overall, Innovest's research is used to screen positively and manage approximately $2.5 billion of invested assets.

Positive screening (that is, investing in companies with superior environmental performance) can be used for stock picking and indexing investment approaches. To illustrate, Dutch pension fund ABP (the world's largest pension fund with $175 billion in assets) is using positive screening to establish two $100 million portfolios, one focused on North American equities and the other on European equities. Innovest's environmental and social research will be combined with traditional financial analysis to guide investments toward environmental and social leaders. ABP's goals include reducing risk exposure, enhancing returns, and improving the environmental performance of its investments.

To illustrate indexing approaches, Dreyfus and Mellon Capital Management launched an eco-enhanced index fund strategy in early 2000. The fund maintains the same sector weightings as its benchmark, the S&P 500, but within sectors, Innovest research is used to overweight environmental leaders and underweight lower rated companies. By shifting investments toward presumably better managed companies, the fund is intended to outperform the S&P 500, which it has done. Figure 3.4 illustrates the structure of the Dreyfus-Mellon fund relative to its benchmark.

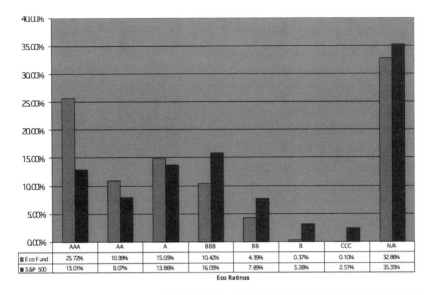

	AAA	AA	A	BBB	BB	B	CCC	N/A
■ Eco Fund	25.72%	10.99%	15.05%	10.43%	4.39%	0.37%	0.10%	32.86%
■ S&P 500	13.01%	8.07%	13.86%	16.09%	7.89%	3.26%	2.51%	35.35%

Eco Ratings

Figure 3.4 Dreyfus Eco-enhanced Index

Future Directions

The main barrier to providing investors with corporate environmental performance information has been the lack of high-quality data. As noted above, data quality is improving in industrialized nations; however, it remains poor in developing countries. The next barrier on the performance information front is likely to be finding the key drivers of environmental performance that differentiate companies. As more firms recognize the financial and strategic value of improving environmental performance, leading-edge environmental management systems and strategies are implemented more frequently. In some sectors, such as European pharmaceuticals, this has already occurred, raising standards broadly and making it difficult to differentiate firms on a corporate environmental performance basis. More refined data, increased disclosure of quantitative impacts, and new analytic tools, however, may continue to permit some differentiation among firms.

To date, corporate environmental performance analysis has usually focused on assessing incremental performance improvements and systems to foster them. As companies adopt leading-edge practices, differentiation on this basis will become more difficult. Given the growing importance of the broader concept of environmental sustainability, an alternative approach is to focus analysis on adoption of visionary strategies, pursuit of large-scale change, and movement toward sustainability. To analyze relative sustainability performance effectively, researchers must understand both the concept of sustainability and the actions required to achieve it.

Sustainability is likely to be the greatest challenge ever faced by business because it implies that management must address an extraordinarily complex set of interconnected issues and concepts. As environmental and other forces compel companies to bear more complete responsibility for their negative environmental and social impacts, sustainability likely will become a central focus of management and a key driver of business success. This, in turn, is likely to cause investment advisors to incorporate the issue more fully into their investment decisions. As evidence continues to mount that environmental performance is financially relevant, not screening for it could become a violation of fiduciary responsibility.

The role of corporations in addressing the challenge to become sustainable is likely to expand significantly for several reasons. Through globalization, privatization, and increasing influence over political processes, corporations are taking on a larger role in society, which implies that they will be called on to play a more central role in sustainability. As pollution and other impacts increase and environmental systems approach limits, and as measurement technology continues to improve, negative corporate impacts will become more obvious, and pressures to mitigate those impacts will increase. And as the necessity to address sustainability from a systems perspective becomes more apparent (meaning recognizing that no part of Earth's system operates in isolation), calls for companies to address their environmental and social impacts more fully will increase.

Providing investors with high-quality information on relative corporate sustainability performance is difficult, in part, because there is no agreed-upon definition of environmental sustainability or the means to achieve it. One method of estimating performance is to develop a theoretical set of actions needed to achieve sustainability, then assess corporate engagement and effectiveness in taking these actions. This requires estimating the responsibility of the corporate sector in achieving sustainability. From a systems perspective, companies affect all aspects of society. As a result, they may be called on increasingly to participate in societal arenas that have not been their traditional focus.

It is unclear whether the bombing of the World Trade Center on September 11, 2001, will affect views on corporate responsibility or the role of corporations in achieving sustainability. However, concerns about security may prompt some companies to assess more fully and mitigate their environmental and social impacts. From an investor's perspective, growing pressures on companies from many different sources may cause sustainability analysis to become as important as more traditional areas of financial and strategic analysis.

Conclusion

The majority of existing research shows that environmental leaders tend to outperform in the stock market. This likely will be true to an even greater degree in the future as companies continue to face growing pressure to improve their environmental and social performance.

Businesses increasingly recognize the importance of environmental performance measurement. Companies around the world currently spend billions of dollars a year on reducing environmental impacts and moving toward sustainability—with growing investments in environmental metrics, accounting, and management systems. Attitudes toward environmental sustainability are diverse, ranging from reactive to proactive. For the most part, proactive companies are those that are best able to address complex, uncertain, and intangible forces affecting their firms effectively. They also are usually leaders in more traditional business areas. As a result, they tend to outperform their competitors in the stock market.

Analysis of corporate environmental performance is used widely in socially responsible investing, but not nearly as broadly by the mainstream investment community. This is changing as a growing number of mainstream firms, such as ABN-AMRO, Dreyfus, Mellon, and Schroders, use environmental performance as an additional factor in assessing stock market potential. As the financial impacts of environmental issues continue to increase, higher quality data on corporate environmental performance will be needed to minimize investor risk exposure and maximize returns.

PART II
CASE STUDIES AND THE PHILANTHROPIC PARADOX

4

COMMUNITY VOICES

A National Initiative to Improve the Health of Underserved Communities

ALLAN J. FORMICOLA, WALID MICHELEN, AND SANDRA HARRIS

Health care and the uninsured has been a major topic in the United States over the past two decades. The distribution of health care to all U.S. citizens has consumed many hours of national media attention. As the cost of health care and the percent of the gross national revenue devoted to health care kept climbing during the 1980s and the 1990s, political leaders at the state and federal levels tried to find solutions to the dual problems of keeping the costs of health care down while covering more of the uninsured.[1] Responses to these dual problems prompted the creation of governmental and non-governmental initiatives; however, failure to enact a broad universal health care system in the United States in the early 1990s gave rise to the incremental approach to covering the uninsured. The idea was to bring care slowly to groups that had no coverage, mainly the working poor. Government and large employers gave encouragement for the managed care movement in the United States as a theoretical way to keep costs down while increasing coverage of health care to more and more Americans. This approach has not proven successful so far in meeting the needs of the uninsured as medical coverage and health care costs are on the rise again.

During this same period of time, the definition of what constitutes good health and what services are needed to attain it expanded. The

United States published health goals for the nation to achieve by
1990, by 2000, and most recently by 2010.[2] We have not achieved the
stated goals for 1990 and for 2000. Recent Surgeon General Reports
indicate that there are major disparities in oral health and mental
health in the nation due to race, ethnicity and poverty. Eliminating
disparities in health care in the absence of a universal health plan is
a difficult problem. Major foundations in the nation interested in
health care issues have placed their attention on different parts of the
health care system from initiatives to assisting hospitals in making the
shift from in-patient care to ambulatory care to reforms in the education of health professions that emphasize cultural awareness and preventive care, as well as in-depth analyses of Medicaid and Medicare
to the costs of prescription drugs. Into this complex environment, the
W. K. Kellogg Foundation conceived of a national program, Community Voices, to deal with health care issues as they impacted on underserved communities in the nation. The Foundation recognized that
the nation's safety net providers were being placed in jeopardy due
to cost cutting. Those individuals facing the most difficulties (such as
the working poor, people of color, the elderly, and the poor in inner
cities and in rural areas) would suffer even greater problems as access
to care, which was already difficult for such individuals to find, became increasingly scarce as providers of last resort faced major financial challenges.

Community Voices: Health Care for the Underserved—A National
Demonstration of Local Visionary Models is a $55 million national
demonstration program of the W. K. Kellogg Foundation. The Foundation's request for proposals (RFPs) contained nine required core
elements:

1. Specific policy targets for informing local and state public
   and marketplace policy;
2. Redesign of the delivery system to increase cost-effectiveness
   while maintaining high quality;
3. Linkages to public health;
4. Involvement of key players (health and non-health) in the
   community;

5. Strong infrastructure for the maintenance of a network of providers, including financial arrangements and information systems;
6. Responsiveness to the community conditions that affect access to care and opportunities for improving community health;
7. Commitment of significant local resources to support the project;
8. Demonstrated readiness to implement and sustain systems change of national caliber; and
9. Performance as a laboratory through which key audiences and constituents for specific approaches and systems change can learn.

Of the more than eighty responses that were received to the RFP, thirteen sites were selected and funded by the Foundation to participate in the national project. The selected sites are:

Asian Health Services, Oakland, CA
California Rural Indian Health Board, Sacramento, CA
Camillus House, Miami, FL
Columbia University, Northern Manhattan Community Voices Collaborative, NY, NY
Denver Health & Hospital Authority, Denver, CO
District of Columbia General Hospital, Washington, DC
El Paso County Hospital District, Thomason General Hospital, El Paso, TX
The Enterprise Foundation, Baltimore, MD
FirstHealth of the Carolinas, Pinehurst, NC
Ingham County Health Department, Lansing, MI
Institute for Health Improvement in Southeast Michigan, Detroit, MI
University of New Mexico Health Sciences Center, Albuquerque, NM
The University System of West Virginia, Charleston, WV

Each of these sites had in common large underinsured or uninsured population groups with limited or no access to care. The Columbia

University site was funded through the School of Dental and Oral Surgery. It was the only site selected in the northeast and the only one selected that had dentistry as the lead partner. (All of the sites have now entered into the fourth year of their five-year projects.) The sites have been brought together on a regular basis by the Kellogg Foundation in order to share experiences and learn from one another. Several major background papers have been prepared by the Foundation to supplement the effort and assist the sites. The Foundation has an external evaluator reviewing the effort and is working to bring out lessons learned.

Community DentCare leads to Community Voices

The Northern Manhattan Community Voices Collaborative (NMCVC) was the outgrowth of a previous project funded by the Kellogg Foundation known as Community DentCare. Community DentCare paved the way for the successful application to the Foundation for a Community Voices initiative in northern Manhattan. Several important lessons were learned in Community DentCare, which were carried over into the NMCVC. They included: (1) the manner in which to build and sustain a collaborative between university and community groups, (2) how to plan and implement major health service initiatives on a communitywide basis, and (3) how to mobilize resources to achieve program goals. A brief summary of Community DentCare provides the backdrop for the Community Voices initiative in northern Manhattan. Northern Manhattan is a federally designated medical and dental shortage area. The health data for the approximately 400,000 residents demonstrates poor health for diseases such as diabetes and cardiovascular disease. Some have described the health status of residents to be almost third world. The neighborhoods have significantly more individuals living at or below the poverty level than other areas of Manhattan.

Community DentCare was designed to respond to a study by the Harlem Prevention Center of the School of Public Health. In the Prevention Center's report of a door-to-door health survey, a lack of access to oral health care was the number one health issue identified by the residents. The dental school at Columbia, located in the Washington Heights section of northern Manhattan, in collaboration with the Harlem Hospital Dental Department, and with the assistance and encouragement of community-based organizations led by the Alianza Dominicana applied for grant funds to undertake a major dental initiative that would lead to a systems change in access to dental treatment and preventive care. Two separate planning committees composed of faculty from the dental school and community representatives came together to deal with the lack of oral health care and the population's high disease rate revealed by pilot studies. One planning committee designed a program for the Washington Heights/Inwood community and the second for the Harlem community. Since each community is culturally different, it was important to have a separate group for each community because each community placed different priorities on which age group to target for the project. In Washington Heights/Inwood, the community groups wished children to be the primary target for the project while in Harlem the residents wished to give equal consideration to both senior citizens as well as children.

The Kellogg Foundation provided a start-up grant for an ambitious project to improve access to treatment in community locations and to add prevention programs in the public schools. The Kellogg Foundation provided a start-up grant of $1.2 million and through a variety of sources another $10 million was raised for the project. The dental school reviewed its mission, strengthening its community service goals and preparing the faculty to assume major new responsibilities for providing care in community-based locations. The following has been accomplished between 1994 and 2001: (1) dental prevention programs joined the School of Public Health Clinics in seven intermediate public schools, (2) a dental van to serve the HeadStart population and local senior centers was purchased in conjunction with the Children's Aid Society, (3) dental facilities were made available in three primary health care facilities in northern Manhattan, and (4) a major new health facility to provide medical and dental care geared to the elderly was constructed in central Harlem.

In 2001 35,000 patient visits in the community were provided, up from only a few thousand in 1994. While implementation of the dental project was well underway, the working relationships built up under Community DentCare became the basis for the application for the broader Community Voices initiative.

The Northern Manhattan Community Voices Collaborative (NMCVC)

The Northern Manhattan Community Voices Collaborative developed its plans to attract a Community Voices site to New York with a broad coalition, expanding the original DentCare partners. The coalition had three lead partners: the Columbia University School of Dental and Oral Surgery, Harlem Hospital Dental Service, and Alianza Dominicana. The three lead partners, who consulted widely within the institutions and in the community, worked out the goals for NMCVC. What emerged was an action-oriented agenda to solve major problems confronting the community and the institutions. Balancing the goals between community needs and desires and institution needs and desires while at the same time responding to the nine core elements was difficult. However, consensus was reached principally because the partners had learned how to work together in the Community DentCare project and each was willing to compromise for the success of the whole. Of great importance was the desire of all to utilize their individual strengths to improve the community. What emerged were four major overlapping goals along the Community Voices mission. The four overlapping goals—if achieved—would move toward systems change. The goals for the NMCVC are: (1) to implement programs to extend community outreach efforts to increase enrollment of residents into existing health insurance programs such as Medicaid and Children's Health Insurance Program (CHIP), (2) to develop a new health insurance product for workers in small businesses in northern Manhattan, (3) to plan and offer health promotion/disease prevention programs, and (4) to provide improved access to hard to cover services, specifically dental and mental health care.

An organizational structure was set up around these four goals, to balance initiatives between community-based organizations and the major health providers including the Health Sciences Schools of

Columbia University and the major hospitals serving northern Manhattan. Over the past four years, the manner in which the partners and collaborators have come together to achieve planning for different initiatives has taken form. A structure exists in which programs get planned and implementation strategies are put into place. The NMCVC understands that it cannot operate programs, but instead the value in its work is to bring the correct groups and individuals together to plan needed initiatives, help find the resources to implement projects, and find the appropriate "home" for the program to reside so that it will be sustained. Finally, the NMCVC understands that in order for systems changes to occur, policy issues must be understood and changed if barriers to progress prevent implementation. A core team assists each of the four work groups assigned to pursue each of the four goals. Over the past three years, much has been accomplished.

Rather than describe the progress of the numerous initiatives underway, it is more important to describe the manner in which the NMCVC brings together the community and institutions around health issues of importance. For example, the collaborative approach to outreach and enrollment initiatives and to designing mental health strategies to improve access provides some insight into how the collaborative works. In the latter initiative, it was recognized that a community-based organization was better suited to take the lead than an institutional partner. Many residents in northern Manhattan were confused by complicated regulations to sign up for existing insurance such as Medicaid and (CHIP). Residents of the communities were distrustful of providing the required sensitive information. Alianza Dominicana, the community-based organization, devised a program to educate community residents on how to enroll residents into existing insurance products and to assist them in accessing necessary care once enrolled. The School of Public Health designed an educational program for the outreach workers. To date over 120 outreach workers, known as *promotoras*, have been educated. This work of the collaborative attracted a New York State grant to facilitate enrollment of residents into the federal/state health insurance programs for those at or within 200 percent of the poverty level. The state recognized the value of having the community-based organization in the lead role in the sign-up process.

Certainly, having more residents with insurance also helps the safety net providers such as the primary care providers and the hospitals. One of the policy issues the collaborative must now confront is a way to finance and sustain the outreach worker model as part of the costs of the health care system.

In the second example of how the collaboration operates, the collaborative convened and promoted a dialogue among consumers, providers, and policymakers in northern Manhattan around the mental health problems in the community. Mental illness is a major and largely unaddressed problem both nationally and in northern Manhattan. Twenty-two key interviews were conducted over a one-year period with local providers of mental health services, with the supportive service providers for mental health consumers and with community activists. With information from these interviews in hand, eight small groups gathered to discuss such issues as barriers to seeking mental health services, including cultural barriers, mental health needs in the community, and resources and capacity required to improve access to services. Existing data from the New York City Department of Mental Health and from the hospitals in the area were reviewed. A report entitled *Mental Health: The Neglected Epidemic*[3] described the problems in northern Manhattan with recommendations on how to improve access to care. The report has been discussed widely in community forums and with institutional leaders. Now, strategic initiatives are being discussed to address the issues.

In both of these examples, the major lesson for community collaboration is to create a harmonious environment of mutual respect in which the interests of both institution and community are represented and in which solutions are balanced to address the concerns of both institution and community. This requires extensive consultation and a keen understanding of the culture of both the institution and the community. Each partner needs to be represented by people committed to the overall mission and goals of the collaborative as well as understanding of the mutual dependence between community and institution. Mutual trust between partners happens when all partners "roll up their sleeves" and work together. The NMCVC strives to function in this manner.

The National Community Voices Network

To assist the thirteen Community Voices sites in their efforts to increase access to health care for vulnerable populations, the Kellogg Foundation contracted with health policy, public relations, and evaluation experts to put together a resource team. While uninsured populations across the nation share similar issues relating to access, the approaches used by each of the thirteen Community Voices sites to address them differ across the country. Understanding these differences, the Foundation views the sites as national "learning laboratories" who are building effective partnerships and promoting dialogue at the local level with the ultimate goal of improving the nation's health care system for the underserved.

Using a learning through sharing approach, the thirteen sites come together to articulate common trends, challenges, and innovative approaches used to address some of the challenges they face. A series of networking/information sharing activities are planned in collaboration with the resource team, Foundation program staff, and the thirteen project directors. This national network provides the various sites with a better understanding of the goals embedded in the Community Voices initiative while at the same time providing multiple venues for the Foundation to assist the work of the sites they funded. Networking across sites takes place at various levels. Communication and relationship building are the key tools utilized to tease out the lessons learned about policy, practice, and systems change. The thirteen sites engage in a deliberate reflective process for learning as they set out to improve the nation's health system to better meet the needs of the underserved. Three mechanisms are utilized:

1. Quarterly conference calls: The Foundation organizes conference calls with each of the sites. Local sites bring together key collaborators to provide updates on progress made around the expected outcomes of their projects. The resource team is available during these calls to provide insight about similar issues arising from various sites. Conference calls are transcribed and used by the resource team to begin to look

for common practices/lessons emerging from local efforts and are shared with the sites.

2. National program directors' meetings: Project directors are brought together to share and discuss the challenges they face in maintaining a collaborative structure in each of the thirteen Community Voices sites. Given that all of the sites have partnered with either a community-based provider, academic and/or medical institutions, discussing and assessing how these partnership come together to promote systems change is among the key factors addressed during these meetings. Directors have an opportunity to hear from their peers on how they have addressed barriers that may hinder the collaborative partners ability to move the work forward.

3. Annual networking conference: The Networking Conference brings together collaborative partners with others in the field working to improve the health care delivery system. The conferences serve as a source of information and motivation for the sites. For example, at the first networking meeting held in 1998, the thirteen funded sites learned about the core element for this project: *Relationships are primary and everything else is secondary.* Understanding that one of the challenges for this national initiative was to build relationships, the sites went forth to bring allies to the table in order to strengthen collaborations to impact systems change at the local and, by example, the national level.

The W. K. Kellogg Foundation encourages the sites to share the lessons they learned at national health care forums and by issuing information about the project through the release of publications about the projects' findings.

To assess the progress made across sites, the Kellogg Foundation has established four broad expected outcomes from this national project. They are that the sites have: (1) sustained an increase in access to health services for the vulnerable with a focus on primary care and prevention, (2) preserved and strengthened safety-net providers in the community, (3) changed delivery systems in which care is delivered in a much more cost-effective way and quality remains high, and

(4) developed best practices that provide examples of different approaches and strategies other communities can select from and adapt to their unique circumstances. This national program enters into its final year in the 2003 year. It is yielding new information and ways for the United States to deal with the difficult issues of providing health care to its most vulnerable residents. The first major publication from Community Voices on the lessons learned has recently been published. It provides insights into the experiences of the various projects across the nation. The report emphasizes the value of reorienting health care systems in underserved communities around primary care and prevention and through collaborations.[4]

5

WORKING TOGETHER

Corporate and Community Development

CAROL GLAZER

This is the story of a partnership between a foundation and a large developer of shopping and entertainment complexes in cities across the country. The purpose of the partnership was to channel job opportunities in the development to residents of communities struggling with high unemployment. This story is about the partners and, in particular, why they came to the table, what happened, and the lessons they learned.

The foundation has had a longstanding interest in work force development, having made grants in the area of research and development and evaluation of employment and training programs, particularly targeted to low-income communities. This partnership was an opportunity for the foundation to help communities organize around a very large real estate development and employment center.

The corporation's typical development has 2 million square feet of space, 200 tenants, and between 3,500 and 4,000 jobs. The developments are huge mega complexes, often open twenty-four hours a day. The developments contain retail, entertainment, restaurants, theme stores, and even places where you can fish. The publicly traded company depends upon public approvals for everything from zoning variances to permits to highway interchanges and environmental clearances. The company also has several enlightened executives who believe seriously in its role as a good corporate citizen and civic leader. In short, the company has many incentives to contribute positively to the communities in which it does business.

The Partnership Emerges

The corporation initially approached the foundation while in the midst of a development project in which it sought to make one-quarter of its jobs available to local residents. The company wanted the foundation to assist it in meeting job commitments. While the partnership never materialized in the first effort, the foundation and corporation began discussing a broader partnership in other cities. In the chosen city, the corporation aimed for a May 2000 grand opening—merely eighteen months after the partnership's inception.

A deal was struck in which the foundation would bring its contacts and its knowledge about work force development and community organizing. The corporation, in turn, would make a very substantial financial commitment, in this case $1.5 million. Together, the two organizations would work in partnership to create a jobs program in the complex for economically disadvantaged workers from the area's lowest income neighborhoods.

The process involved an extensive amount of community organizing, work with state and local government and employment and training organizations, resolution of transportation and childcare issues and other barriers to work for poor and excluded job seekers.

This was not a popular project within either organization. For the corporation, a lot of people saw this partnership with a philanthropic organization as potentially costly, time consuming, and certainly not guaranteed to produce any business results. This was especially true in the development division, where time is money and deadlines are tracked with the precision of a NASA countdown.

From the foundation's point of view, these were low-paying, often part-time jobs in the retail sector, often perceived as dead end jobs. Why should the foundation put its good name and its resources behind something that didn't produce good jobs with family sustaining wages?[1]

These obstacles notwithstanding, both the foundation and the corporation moved forward given the huge upside potential in community benefits.

Partnership Outcomes

The foundation and corporation entered into a partnership that sought to recruit, train, and provide career advancement opportunities for one thousand job seekers from two targeted neighborhoods, the city's poorest census tracts. That goal was met by opening day.

The centerpiece of the partnership's work was a 4,000-square foot "employee learning and development center" that the corporation built and outfitted as part of the retail development. The center provides job readiness and skills training and works with employers to customize its training to their needs. The corporation made a tandem $300,000 commitment to the city's local "one stop" employment agency to operate the learning center.

The partnership also secured funding from the Federal Transit Authority (FTA) under its "reverse commute" program, in which buses were re-routed and schedules changed to get workers from the city to the suburbs (the opposite direction of buses in this "hub and spoke" system emanating from the city to the suburbs); and to accommodate the extended hours of the shopping complex. Through a childcare component, the partnership secured seventy-five subsidized slots in a childcare center abutting the development. Finally, of most interest to the foundation, both the foundation and the corporation supported a three-year very intensive community organizing effort in the neighborhoods from which the partnership sought to recruit workers.

In the end, this unique partnership succeeded, and both partners learned a great deal from their work together.

Questions Raised and Lessons Learned

This case raises a number of intriguing questions. First of all: Is this or in what ways was this really a partnership? A second question: Does this kind of partnership work and, if so, under what conditions? And third: Is it worthwhile? These questions all have the same answer: Yes, but only under certain conditions.

The word partnership, derives from the Latin root: "partior" to share, divide, take part in. Most partnerships involve very explicit agreements in which control, expenses, rewards, and exposure are divided in fixed proportion according to each partner's investment and according to each partner's risk. This case had no explicit agreements. On the contrary, it had only general goals and understandings about each partner's role.

For example, the foundation wanted to serve poor, disenfranchised communities, in part by bringing employment opportunities to excluded job seekers. The corporation wanted to build political good will and show good corporate citizenship. And a third partner, the leadership of the city, wanted to maximize jobs for unemployed residents. In summary, no partner had the same number one priority goal. But these differences notwithstanding, the partnership worked, since: (1) no participant had interests that were *at odds* with the others, that is, there were no serious conflicts in the fundamental goals of each partner; (2) a couple of very significant goals were common to the partners, especially the desire to bring opportunities to disenfranchised people and develop their connections to employers; and (3) no one partner could have done this on its own.

Herein are the major conditions that must be satisfied for a successful partnership of this kind:

Lesson One: Partners' priority goals need not be the same but they cannot conflict.

Lesson Two: Both partners must be willing to accept a degree of exposure, both financial and reputational. Senior executives at both the foundation and the corporation recognized the potential risks and accepted a fair amount of public exposure. They did so because of the huge potential upside of employing one thousand people who wouldn't otherwise have access to jobs in the development. This exposure, borne in good supply by both parties, cemented the partnership and the parties' commitment to ensuring its success.

Lesson Three: More important than formal explicit agreements are a high level of commitment, goodwill, trust and close working relationships among partners. For all that this partnership lacked in explicit agreements, players not only had a lot on the line, they also both made a commitment to work together closely. They also developed a high level of trust and goodwill; and good working relationships on the ground among the staff members charged with implementing the project. Overall, the corporation and the foundation made it through some difficult situations together, with a very strong bond and working relationship. In that sense, this was a partnership at its best.

Lesson Four: The corporation should have a freely acknowledged business need to be involved: a desire merely to support a project as an outgrowth of corporate charity is positive, but not enough. As a publicly traded commercial real estate developer, the corporation depends upon public approvals for nearly every aspect of its operations; its executives are among the most politically savvy in the business. The positive public relations generated by the company's participation in the partnership translated into bottom line business benefits that were lost on no one. Had this been about corporate philanthropy alone, the corporation would not have made the necessary investment of time and money to ensure project success.

Lesson Five: People at every level of the corporation should see the benefits of being involved. The corporation had to get its hands dirty. For that to work people at every single level of the organization have to believe in the project; and the belief had to be strong and preferably rooted in first-hand experience.

In this case, only the development director and the executive vice president were seriously committed, but not anyone else in the company, including and especially the leasing people, the single most important element, since they deal with tenant employers. To win their acceptance, the partnership offered something that tenant businesses needed, that is, trained, ready-to-work employees. The partnership capitalized on this through moves that had a way of cascading to get the leasing people, and ultimately others in the company, bought in at every level.

Lesson Six: The company's role in the activity should derive from things the company already does well. The same goes for the foundation. The partnership didn't seek to develop new expertise or new social passions among people in the company. It focused on development, building up the learning and development center, and focused on hiring, which is something very familiar to this company and its tenants. The same can be said for the foundation, with respect to the work force development system and community organizing. In each case, partners applied themselves to things they do in the course of doing business: things they understand it, things they know, and things under the command of the true believers, all of whom were cultivated in the process of getting this done.

Lesson Seven: The company has to be very comfortable in the public spotlight, very deft at dispelling controversy, and eager for public attention. This case involved a high level of visibility for both partners, and in some cases, taking public positions on political issues. If the company was scared by the possibility of occasional disputes with government, skeptical community people, or skeptical press coverage, the project could never have gone forward.

In this case a major business partner and a philanthropic institution, in the end, developed a very real partnership with some very significant lessons. The results speak for themselves.

Conclusion

In the end, this unique partnership between a significant profit-making business and a philanthropic foundation achieved all that it set out to do. By opening day, more than one thousand people from Nashville's lowest income neighborhoods had jobs at the development. Transit was re-routed to accommodate residents' "reverse commute" (city to suburbs) needs. Day care arrangements were made for many working parents who needed them. And a 3,000-square foot Employee Learning and Development Center ensures that these supports—as well as opportunities for career advancement—can be sustained over time, reaching future generations of workers.

The initial questions about whether this was really a partnership, whether it worked, and whether it was worth it, can all be answered with an unequivocal YES. And as is often the case in complex transactions among multiple parties, the reasons are subtle and idiosyncratic, often reduced to superb working relationships among people charged with the work on the ground. But there's more to this story, a set of lessons that can be applied to similar institutional relationships among unlikely partners.

6

LATINO NONPROFITS

The Role of Intermediaries
in Organizational Capacity Building

AIDA RODRIGUEZ, JOSEPH A. PEREIRA,
AND SHANA BRODNAX

It is generally agreed that within the nonprofit sector there is insufficient attention paid to organizational capacity building. Letts, Ryan, and Grossman (1999) argue that this deficiency stems, in part, from the fact that the focus in the nonprofit sector has been on the development of new programmatic initiatives and expanding existing programs to new markets with little reward for building organizational capacity (8). To remedy what they say is widespread weakness in the area of organizational capacity, they correctly suggest that nonprofits should invest in management processes that "enhance responsiveness to clients and support quality improvements . . . and build on nonprofit assets without compromising commitment to social goals" (201).

In this chapter, we provide a summary of the major capacity building needs of nonprofits, relying on findings from a recently completed survey of Latino nonprofits on the East Coast including Miami, Florida. As organizing principles, we use three major categories of need introduced by Letts, Ryan, and Grossman (1999): (1) program delivery capacity, (2) program expansion capacity, and (3) adaptive capacity. Next, we examine the roles that intermediaries currently play in helping nonprofits achieve organizational health and provide examples of what some intermediaries are doing to support smaller nonprofits. Finally, we consider the challenges and opportunities in expanding the role of intermediaries so that they can meet the needs of more nonprofits. We are well aware of the fact that changes in the nonprofit sector (including intermediaries) referred to in this chapter are taking place globally (Salamon et al., 1999), but we will focus on the nonprofit sector in the United States.

At a time when the nonprofit sector is facing new challenges including increased competition from within and outside the sector, it is essential that nonprofits—the majority of which are small and fragile financially—use intermediaries as allies in both responding to the demands on the sector and in the enormous task of capacity building.

The aim of this chapter is not to provide a comprehensive review of the significant literature available on the capacity building needs of the nonprofit sector, nor does it go beyond a cursory review of the services offered by the handful of intermediaries reviewed. Rather, the goal is to report on what executive directors of nonprofits say is important for organization's health, to analyze the capacities of selected intermediaries, and to stimulate some thought about the kinds of strategies that might strengthen the growing partnership between these two types of entities. In addition to survey data concerning Latino nonprofits, secondary documents and a review of web site content, Aida Rodriguez relies on a decade of experience and observations as an officer of a major U.S. international private foundation.[1]

The Changing Environment

Elizabeth Boris (1999) reports that in 1996 the nonprofit sector "consisted of approximately 1.5 million organizations, including all tax-exempt organizations registered with the IRS and 341,000 religious congregations that are eligible for tax deductible contributions but are not required to register with the government" (6). She adds that "the independent sector expanded with the economy over the last two decades. Its percentage of the national income rose from 4.9 percent in 1977 to 6.2 percent in 1996" (9) "with an estimated $621.4 billion in revenues in 1996" (6). She cautions, however, that the "independent sector's share of the national income decreased between 1992 and 1996, despite continued growth in the number of voluntary organizations" (9).

Besides changes in the number of nonprofits, organizations today are operating in a new and complex environment characterized by rapid political and social change. For example, there are more demands on nonprofit organizations to serve client populations that are more culturally diverse than they were in the recent past and to respond to calls for accountability, including program evaluation. Also, organizations face increased competition from both within and outside the sector. Specifically, new organizations compete with more established ones for limited funding, and *all* nonprofits must compete with private for-profit organizations that now provide services in areas traditionally considered the domain of the nonprofit sector. In short, grants, government contracts, and fees—which have been the mainstay of nonprofit income—are now sought competitively by more and newer nonprofits that often replicate services provided by more established firms and by private companies providing similar services.

The passage in 1996 of both the Personal Responsibility and Work Opportunity and Reconciliation Act, the Illegal Immigration Reform and Immigration Responsibility Act, and subsequent changes in major housing and jobs legislation have resulted in the devolution of responsibility for implementation of policy from the federal level to state and local levels. The result has been an opening of new opportunities for local nonprofits. Nonprofits can now provide government services that were previously not within their purview. But they must compete—often with other nonprofits and increasingly with large private sector organizations. In short, policy changes have worked to change radically the environment within which the clients of nonprofits live and, in turn, increase the demands they place on the nonprofit sector.

In a recent study of organizations serving immigrants in New York City, Cordero-Guzman and Navarro (2000) report that the organizations "have had to spend more time doing public education and advocacy on behalf of the organization, its services and their clients" (26), as well as providing free food, greater assistance with completing complicated paperwork, and other basic services. In addition, the time limits placed on welfare recipients have put pressure on nonprofits to help low-income individuals prepare for jobs.

One of the biggest challenges posed by changes in federal and local policies is that nonprofits are being forced to keep abreast of the new policy environment—getting informed and staying informed is now critical to survival. As we argue later in this chapter, accumulating and distributing relevant policy and practical information (e.g., providing information about best practices) is an important role to be played by large intermediaries.

Demographic shifts in the nation's urban (and increasingly rural) areas are also impacting the nonprofit sector. For example, the number of Latinos living in the United States has tripled over the last two decades to approximately 30 million. By the year 2005, Latinos will be the nation's largest minority (Campoamor and Diaz, 1999). By the year 2050, one out of four residents will be Latinos (U.S. Bureau of the Census, 1997)—making Latinos the largest panethnic group in the United States. Consider also that Latinos are just one part of a huge wave of immigration that has altered the face of American cities. In New York City, for example, there are sizeable numbers of Russians, Chinese, Asian Indians, and Bangladeshi immigrants. The result is that there is now enormous pressure on nonprofits not only to respond to more people with new needs but also new immigrants with cultures different from those that have been traditionally served by nonprofits. This means that managers have to know how to negotiate across ethnic and racial boundaries and across national identities. Some of the most innovative organizations think of themselves as "transnational" or organizations that "cross borders." Indeed, a number of Latino scholars have written on the subject of transnational cultural identities and the role of civil society organizations in addressing the issues posed by this reality (Bonilla et al., 1998). The fact is that in response to a global economy and thus a global work force, nonprofits must now reach across borders in much the same way multinational corporations have done for years.

Further complicating the context for nonprofits are major changes taking place within the philanthropic sector. In particular, there has been a growth of "big money" donors who not only want to make decisions regarding how their money is being "invested" (Billitteri, 2000), but also want to influence directly the missions of organizations. There is also a trend toward raising and donating funds through the Internet, thereby changing older established notions of fund raising and gift giving.

The bottom line is that those operating in the nonprofit sector today need to be smart, informed, versatile, and accountable. This results in greater demands for strong management and organizational skills—that is, the development of organizational capacity. However, for most nonprofits, developing these skills is not only expensive but also is all too often quite difficult.

Capacity Building: What Are the Needs?

The needs of nonprofits are as varied as the sector itself, but there are core elements that researchers say are required to make an organization function properly. Letts, Ryan, and Grossman (1999) find that effective nonprofit organizations demonstrate effectiveness in three major areas of organizational capacity: (1) program delivery, (2) program expansion, and (3) adaptive capacity. The third, adaptive capacity, is what makes an organization not only efficient but also effective (19–20).

In this section, we rely on three sources of information to provide a broad overview of the capacity building needs of nonprofits. The first are data from a recently completed survey of 336 Latino nonprofits on the East Coast. The study was completed by the Puerto Rican Legal Defense Fund (PRLDEF), under contract to Hispanics in Philanthropy (HIP).[2] In addition to the survey data, information was collected from two focus group sessions with nonprofit leaders conducted in New York City, New Jersey, and Connecticut.

The second source of information consists of observations and information contained in an interim report summarizing findings from *Next Steps: Jobs Initiative*, funded by the Rockefeller Foundation. *Next Steps* was implemented between 1995–1998 by the Corporation for Supportive Housing (CSH) and twenty nonprofit providers in Chicago, the San Francisco Bay Area, and New York City. The purpose of this initiative was to enhance employment opportunities for the tenants of supportive housing.

We supplement these two sources with information from the Hispanic Federation of New York on what their sixty-six members claim are their capacity building needs.

Program Delivery Capacity

Program delivery capacity requires that an organization have the necessary organizational and management skills to deliver a service or program effectively (Letts, Ryan, and Grossman, 1999, 20). Several needs were most prominent among the nonprofits reviewed: (1) strategic and program planning and human resource development, (2) revenue generation, and (3) technological development. These areas were also cited where technical assistance was sought the most often.

Planning and Human Resources The Corporation for Supportive Housing and the twenty collaborating nonprofits decided to move forward with *Next Steps: Jobs Initiative* only after one year of evidence gathering, strategic planning, and individual program planning. They found that delivering new employment services to residents of supportive housing required organizations to prepare for the implementation of a new program and to make significant changes in their internal workings. Staff members had to be trained and retrained to understand the objectives of the employment programs. In most cases successful implementation required significant change in the organizational culture. This meant changing the way people in these organizations were served—including identifying and training staff to share a common mission. For example, this meant that key to a successful outcome was deploying staff members at sites who were dedicated to helping residents develop skills, find jobs, and remain employed. This was a difficult task that at times required hiring and training new staff and moving some existing staff to new positions within the organizations. It also meant paying attention to the motivational needs of the staff members on the front lines (Corporation for Supportive Housing [CSH], 1997). Consider that the PRLDEF survey showed that, for the sample as a whole, the most serious problem facing organizations was the inability to attract qualified personnel. The organizations claim that they need qualified personnel to develop relationships with funding sources and help with strategic planning. However, the Latino organizations studied find it difficult to attract individuals that can help fund raise. Also, the executive directors of these Latino organizations do not have the time and resources to make long-term strategic plans. These two factors are related. Lack of funds pose an additional problem—that is, having difficulty paying the cost of employee health benefits and pensions (Pereira and Ronda, 2000).

Consistent with these reports are the observations made by the Hispanic Federation that many Latino organizations are growing quickly, in response to increased immigration, but are doing so without the benefit of strategic planning and with little time to retrain or hire new staff (Hispanic Federation, 2000).

Revenue Generation   For the Latino nonprofits, the second serious capacity need is the ability to secure core funds to operate the organization adequately. An analysis of the problems experienced by Latino organizations indicates that the percent of administrative overhead allowed in government contracts is directly related to securing core funds to operate the organization (Pereira and Ronda, 2000).

Another priority for these organizations is to increase the ability of the board to raise funds. In the focus group sessions, directors of the Latino nonprofits indicated that founding board members were instrumental in starting the organization but as the organization changes over time, these same board members are not skilled in the art of fund raising.

A major problem reported by Latino directors is related to the negative impact of government funding on the organizations' cash flow. Some organizations say that having to provide multiple services in order to secure enough funding is a serious problem. It is likely that the impact of rules and regulations for obtaining government funding and maintaining adequate levels of services are serious problems as well.

That revenue generation is a major concern is also demonstrated by the consistent request for training in proposal writing and for access to potential funders by the PRLDEF survey respondents (Pereira and Ronda, 2000).

Evidence from the CSH demonstration showed that creating and expanding businesses run for the purpose of training and hiring supportive housing residents was key. Some providers, like Rubicon Programs in California, already operated successful enterprises before the *Next Steps* demonstration, but their sales increased from

$270,000 to almost $900,000 in two years. Total combined gross revenues for the social purpose ventures operated by the providers exceeded $10 million. The nonprofits needed social entrepreneurial expertise (CSH, 1997).

Technological Development   Close to one-third of the PRLDEF respondents indicated that acquiring adequate computer technology was a "very serious" problem. Yet, only 16 percent of the respondents had received any computer or technology assistance (Pereira and Ronda, 2000), and the percentage was less than 10 percent in New Jersey and Connecticut where the need for assistance was greatest (Pereira and Ronda, 2000). The request for technological assistance is also a priority for the executive directors of the Hispanic Federation member agencies (Hispanic Federation, 2000). Note that the problem is not one of simply buying a computer but rather is related to not having the resources to network an organization's computers, install and maintain software adequate to the task of managing the organization's databases, and finally training staff on the use of the software.

Program Expansion Capacity

There is a constant demand among nonprofits for assistance as they take on new responsibilities—not just a planned expansion but in their growing need to respond to a changing client base and new political context. Letts, Ryan, and Grossman (1999) emphasize that "with more staff, funders, and sites, more formal systems are needed to handle payroll, financial control, promotion, and program documentation. Fundraising needs to be handled deliberately and strategically" (20). The strong demand for skills to enable nonprofits to build strong collaborations fits into this category.

Financial Management Skills   In the PRLDEF study, directors of Latino nonprofits were asked to rate a list of services and forms of technical assistance with respect to how useful each would be in addressing some organizational need. Sixty-nine percent of the Latino nonprofits responded that help with developing their accounting system would be useful. A sizeable majority (76%) reported that having an outside firm handle their payroll operation would be a useful service for their organization (Pereira, 2000).

Brokering Evidence from the Rockefeller Foundation demonstration and the Latino Nonprofits Study confirms the importance of the need for organizational leaders to develop brokering skills—learning how to be players and partners is key to survival. Forming connections between residents of supportive housing and effective off-site employment and training services proved to be very important to the success of an organization. CSH and the local nonprofits had to equip and train staff to identify important outside resources and how to broker a relationship with them. An example of this is developing ongoing relationships with employers to persuade them that it is in their own interest to hire supportive housing residents. The nonprofits and CSH need the skills to negotiate and create win-win situations with the private sector.

The PRLDEF report added questions about problems associated with collaborations and mergers only after the directors in the New York City focus group voiced considerable concern about implementing collaborations and executing mergers. Concerns regarding strategic alliances are widespread as evidenced by the fact that 75 percent of the executive directors reported that the establishment of an intermediary that could plan and coordinate collaborations and mergers would be very useful to them. Whether the directors say they find this a useful service because they are being asked to form such linkages or because as some directors indicated during the focus group that collaboration is a way of enabling Latino organizations to survive depends on the director being asked the question (Pereira and Ronda, 2000). The motivation in many cases is a combination of both these two factors. In any case, the directors said during the focus group session that in their experience, arranging collaborations, mergers, and other linkages are complicated and time consuming. Moreover, it is an effort that requires additional trained personnel to plan and execute.

In summary, there is ample evidence in both the CSH demonstration and the PRLDEF study, that for nonprofits, large and small, to respond to the changes in their client base and to broad changes in policy, they need to have specific skills. Staff members have to be able to plan strategically and managers need to be able to identify staff members' skills and to change and rotate them as needed. They need staff that can broker across sectors, consider businesses, and pursue for-profit ventures. They need to have or be able to find social entrepreneurial expertise.

Adaptive Capacity

Letts, Ryan, and Grossman (1999) define adaptive capacity as "the processes that support a different set of organizational goals, including: "Learning: to measure performance and identify both problems and possibilities for improvements; Responsiveness: to understand how well clients are served and what changes need to be made to improve the quality of service; Innovativeness: to use the organization's people and knowledge to create new programs: and Motivation: to create jobs and organizations where staff and volunteers see the results of their work—the foundation for motivating people" (21). They argue that nonprofits must use management processes that build on "distinctive nonprofit assets" which include "commitment to service, teamwork, and employee empowerment" (201).

What is most telling is what little is said in the literature we reviewed about the need within Latin nonprofits for a capacity to develop an adaptive environment. We believe this reflects the fact that many Latino agencies are understaffed and thus, staff priorities reflect the day-to-day needs of providing services and organizational survival. For example, half the PRLDEF study respondents mention that they have a "very serious" problem paying salaries that attract qualified personal but less than one-fifth of the organizations indicate that they received any kind of technical assistance for staff development and training—activities that would sustain and enhance the work of the existing staff. The list of "very serious" problems presented by the organizations typically focus on the practical, immediate needs—such as fund raising—and less so on developing teamwork and empowering employees. The one exception is the mention (from 30 percent of the organizations) that the lack of time for long-term strategic planning is a "very serious" problem—a critical aspect of creating an adaptive capacity (Pereira and Ronda, 2000).

Accessing Knowledge and Agenda Setting   There was also little mention of two other activities that fit under the rubric of adaptive capacity building, particularly adapting to a changing context: accessing knowledge and agenda setting. As we stated earlier, there is a growing necessity for organizations to understand globalization trends, changes in domestic policy, and best practices from the field. In addition, nonprofits must be able to understand and measure their own outcomes and program impact. The ability to do both requires nonprofit managers to know how to access, use information management tools, and maintain effective systems of accountability. Nonprofits must be able to reach out into new fields, such as work force development, thereby requiring that they learn how to set new agendas in response to the changes in the external context. For both of these sets of activities, the role of the intermediaries appears particularly important.

Meeting the Needs: The Role of Intermediaries

Among intermediaries, most of which are nonprofits themselves, the best are wizards at brokering, gathering, analyzing, and sharing information. Their strengths are one reason why they receive substantial financial support from national and local foundations, corporate philanthropists, and private donors to help other nonprofits with support. The good news is that in the last two decades there has been an increase in the number of national, state, and local intermediaries. In short, small nonprofits do not have to go it alone, but *all* managers need to know at least how to identify and access these intermediaries.

Earlier we identified the major areas of capacity building need: strategic planning, program planning, effective management of human resources and leadership development, access to capital and revenue generation, technological development, financial management, building partnerships and strong collaborations, accessing knowledge and performance measurement, and agenda setting and performance measurement. A cursory review of selected web sites and general documentation from the major housing and community development intermediaries and one ethnic-specific fund, the Hispanic Federation, shows that the intermediaries are reaching out to nonprofits to help them meet the capacity building needs of the nonprofit sector. Following is a summary of some of the major assistance provided. This quick review of these selected intermediaries is meant to highlight some of the different kinds of services and tools intermediaries are providing to the nonprofit sector.

Housing and Community Development Intermediaries

In summary, the assistance in capacity building offered by housing and community development intermediaries focuses on the following broad categories:

- Providing access to grants, loans and equity
- Housing development and management, which can include program planning and administration, asset and property management, and production
- Nonprofit management technical assistance, which can include strategic planning, board governance, fund raising, and financial management
- Assisting CDCs to expand their agendas beyond housing to include employment, child care, community security, and other issues of importance to low-income communities
- Documentation and dissemination information on best practices
- Public education and advocacy

Local Initiatives Support Corporation   The Local Initiatives Support Corporation (LISC), with headquarters in New York City, provides grants, loans, and equity investments to community development corporations (CDCs) for neighborhood redevelopment. LISC has two affiliates that attract additional private capital for CDCs: (1) the National Equity Fund, Inc.—the nation's largest nonprofit syndicator of low-income housing tax credits and (2) the Retail Initiative—which helps design large-scale retail developments (www.liscnet.org, September 2000).

LISC also offers a number of national programs that assist CDCs in brokering effective partnerships—for example, the Community Security Initiative (partnership with local police), the Housing Authority Resource Center (building partnerships with local housing authorities), and Community Investment Collaborative for Kids (developing community partnerships for child care).

In addition, with support from funders in the National Community Development Initiative (NCDI),[3] LISC supports nonprofits in capacity building through its Organizational Development Initiative (ODI). ODI is LISC's "in-house management consultant, providing a broad array of services and technical assistance to CDCs. A national program based in New York City, ODI designs locally delivered trainings and business tools for improving both day-to-day operations and strategic thinking and planning." ODI resources increase the capacity of CDCs in the following areas: "asset and property management; real estate development; program administration; legal structure, board governance, management information systems, financial management, personal policy administration, and mission and strategy" (www.liscnet.org, September 2000). LISC also assists CDCs in expanding their services through national initiatives focusing on issues such as jobs and income.

The Enterprise Foundation   The Enterprise Foundation (TEF) also provides grants, loan, and equity investments to CDCs. Like LISC it has national programs, as well as local offices. It too has a private subsidiary, Enterprise Social Investment Corporation, to help package equity financing for nonprofits from private investors.

On the direct management side, it supplies nonprofits with one-on-one expertise, dispensed through its local offices. TEF aids CDCs in housing development and management—including program planning, financing development projects (including putting together bank consortiums, designing a housing trust, etc.), production, property, and asset management. TEF provides specific services and tools to help nonprofits develop management skills in planning, governance, money management, fund raising, and communications. In addition, the TEF web site is also an excellent resource for policy relevant data. A major initiative of the intermediary is the Community Employment Alliance (CEA). Through CEA, Enterprise works with local job training and placement organizations, businesses, government agencies, and other community-based organizations to improve the quality of employment services for low-income individuals. Tools and activities used by CEA include one-to-one technical assistance, group training, online work force tools in the Enterprise Resource Database, individual employer job initiatives and other activities (www.enterprisefoundation.org, September 2000).

Seedco   Seedco assists community development organizations to undertake social and economic development projects through partnership with anchor institutions such as hospitals, universities and the private sector. Its emphasis is on building strong sustainable partnerships. Seedco and its subsidiary the Non-Profit Assistance Corporation (N-PAC) conduct a needs assessment, then use a capacity building approach that incorporates the development of nonprofit management expertise and strategic planning in the form of the Performance Measurement and Management (PM&M) Process. The PM&M Process focuses on a business plan that uses outcome data to measure progress and improve. Seedco emphasizes helping nonprofits build their management, planning and leadership capacity. Seedco is now conducting and plans to expand its Community Development Technology Initiative, which uses four to eight pilot sites to research and analyze the role of information technology in the work of community revitalization (www.seedco.org, September 2000).

Corporation for Supportive Housing   The Corporation for Supportive Housing (CSH) supports the expansion of service-supported permanent housing for individuals coping with extreme poverty and mental illness, addiction, HIV/ADIS, and other chronic health problems. CSH works with a network of 259 nonprofit providers—similar to other housing intermediaries—to assist these organizations by facilitating access to financial and technical assistance and engaging projects in experiments to test new models, including effective strategies for providing employment services to tenants of supportive housing, information dissemination, and advocacy (www.csh.org, September 2000).

In addition, all four housing and community development intermediaries play a prominent role in advocating for national, state, and local legislation (e.g., the Low Income Housing Tax Credit) and policies that further the mission of CDCs.

Ethnic-Specific Fund: The Hispanic Federation   The Hispanic Federation, a membership organization of sixty-six Latino health and social service organizations in the New York City region, was established by a group of Latino leaders in 1990 after a study conducted by the United Way of New York revealed that, although the need for health and human services was higher for Hispanics than for any other group in New York City, the proportion of government and philanthropic resources allocated to the Latino community was not commensurate with its size. The Federation works to correct this imbalance through three strategies: Fund Development/Grant Making, Technical Assistance Services, and Advocacy (Hispanic Federation, 2000).

A review of the Hispanic Federation web site shows that it delivers technical assistance to its member agencies through the Hispanic Enterprises Launching Programs (HELP) in an effort to build their organizational capacity. HELP concentrates its efforts on the following areas: strategic planning, program development, legal assistance, proposal writing, management training, and technological development. These services include providing small grants and fellowships to their member nonprofit agencies to develop their organizational capacity (www.hispanicfederation.org, September 2000).

Challenges and New Directions

The proceeding summary of the major activities engaged in by intermediaries suggests that they *are* providing much of the type of training and information that nonprofits say they need. It may, therefore, make sense to identify the strategies for strengthening the relationship between intermediaries and the nonprofit sector they have targeted to assist. We turn to that issue now.

National private foundations are strong supporters of intermediaries. In fact, foundations are often the founders of intermediary institutions. Several major explanations for the benevolent attitude of foundations toward intermediaries follow.

1. Intermediaries focus on specific subsectors of the nonprofit sector (CDCs, supportive housing providers, Latino organizations) or specific thematic concerns (poverty, community building, homelessness). Thus, they are able to gain an in-depth knowledge of a field and/or target constituency—a greater knowledge than many philanthropists (who have to be generalists) feel they have. Foundations feel intermediaries can often be more informed about the needs of non-profits and make more informed choices about the best dispersion of funds and technical assistance.

2. Intermediaries, as representatives of a collaboration of smaller nonprofits, can access information about a sector's needs and serve as advocates for policy change as necessary.

3. Intermediaries can take advantage of economies of scale, such as better medical benefits for their staff.

4. They are larger institutions than most nonprofits and as such can better financially manage large-scale grants—a characteristic foundations seek when they want to disperse grant money in the form of large grants.

Thus, intermediaries can serve as a repository of millions in grant dollars—something smaller nonprofits are unable to do. With the increase in philanthropic capital, the ability to attract and manage large-size grants has become important.

From the perspective of the smaller nonprofits, what are the advantages? Intermediaries can serve as a convener of like-minded entities or provide access to a large network of entities. They can facilitate an exchange of information and create an intellectual exchange, sharing information about best practices, lessons from the field, and policy updates. They can be a repository of practitioner and policy-relevant information. They can also provide professional expertise that can benefit smaller nonprofits—that is, in technology, financial management, fund raising, grants management, and strategic planning. Moreover, they can open doors or introduce nonprofits to potentially important allies and partners—that is, banks, foundation officers, other nonprofits. They can help provide access to difficult to get grant funds or in some cases, loans and government subsidies. Intermediaries can take advantage of economies of scale—providing access to group health insurance, discounts on computers, and the like.

Nevertheless, for all the value the intermediaries bring to the various fields in which they operate there are at least three major challenges that impede the intermediaries from achieving maximum impact in their particular domains, which are: (1) nonprofits' lack of access to intermediaries, (2) funder ignorance, and (3) limited sharing of learning. We discuss each of these below and suggest some potential solutions.

Lack of Access to Intermediaries

Not everyone has knowledge of or easy access to what an intermediary has to offer. Small, emerging, or troubled nonprofits—those most in need of the services of an intermediary—are the least likely to know of their existence or feel they can access the help. Two-thirds of the East Coast Latino nonprofits surveyed said they had never received technical assistance. Yet, the five intermediaries we discuss in this chapter and a multitude of nonprofit support organizations and technical assistance providers are based on the East Coast. Moreover, 75 percent indicated that the establishment of an intermediary that could plan and coordinate collaborations and mergers would be useful—an activity that many existing intermediaries now claim they do. Many also mentioned the need for training seminars about policy development and legislative changes—again something intermediaries are already doing. There are various possible explanations for the lack of a connection between existing resources and the demand for services. For one, there may not be enough services and resources available—in other words, there is not enough to go around. The managers may also feel they do not have the time to take advantage of available services. In fact, the Hispanic Federation reports that this is a major problem among their member agencies (Hispanic Federation, 2000). These are certainly important variables to consider. But the problem is complicated by other factors, namely: limited networks and lack of cultural sensitivity and convenience.

The majority of intermediaries rely on the Internet, conferences, targeted initiatives, newsletters, and word of mouth to reach a large network of nonprofits—it is, after all, in their interest to do so. They have the burden of finding those who can use their services. They have less time and money to reach out to those networks with which they are not familiar. In the case of Latino nonprofits—and other nonprofits that reach a well-defined yet new nonprofit subsector—this means that the large intermediaries are not part of the network that these nonprofits turn to for help. Further, executive directors and managers of the nonprofits may not feel that the intermediary is sensitive to the particular cultural issues that they confront. Many Latino agencies are growing quickly without the benefit of strategic planning. The Hispanic Federation summarized the major management training needs of Hispanic institutions as rooted in the following issues (Hispanic Federation, 2000):

- The youthfulness of most Latino organizations. Many agencies are still led by the founder—they have not obtained the additional education to learn new management skills. Succession planning is haphazard.
- The dearth of culturally competent technical assistance opportunities for managers of Latino nonprofits is a major problem (Hispanic Federation, 2000). Latino nonprofit directors or senior managers want to feel that the intermediary not only cares about housing or employment but also that it is sensitive to the particular history and needs of Latinos in the community. Reaching out with sensitivity—for example, making materials accessible in Spanish or by radio or better yet, making formal contact with the organization—is key. The intermediaries need to consider how to use advisory committees or focus groups of representatives of targeted audiences to make the connection to these communities. In addition, they need to provide more services in ways that motivate—and reward—very busy executives and their orga-

nizations to participate. The rewards cannot be individual but rather must be organizational in most cases.

· Another problem is the cost of accessing the available services. Small and financially strapped organizations feel that they cannot afford to pay for the services that intermediaries provide. As a response to the cost question, the Hispanic Federation has raised funds to provide fellowships to managers willing to make the effort to obtain the management training they need. Funders must go beyond simply funding the intermediaries to provide a technical service; they must fund nonprofits themselves to use the services—which in some cases means hiring personnel in order to free a staff member to attend assistance sessions. Funding has to go beyond fellowships to programs that culminate in individual and organizational rewards. For example, accessing management training or attending management workshops should result in certificates, degrees, or involvement in professional networks that can help individuals advance their careers. Training should permit an organization to go beyond one-shot assistance—if an organization gets help in completing a strategic assessment plan they should have funds to implement the plan created. They must also be able to train staff at different levels of the organization. The training must not be only available for the executives but also for all levels of the organization. The assistance has to have short- and long-term implications.

Funder Ignorance

Funders first need to give priority to the development of organization capacity and move away from the sole emphasis on proper project implementation. Second, they need to be part of an open exchange or dialogue between intermediaries and the nonprofits they serve. Intermediaries need to establish—on a regular basis—open forums where their funders and the nonprofits serviced can share the values and weaknesses of capacity building programs that have been established. These can be simple focus groups held at the foundation offices once or twice year. They can follow similar exchanges between the intermediaries and nonprofits themselves. Those invited to the open forums should include those who can benefit from the technical assistance but so far have not done so—an opportunity to listen, be heard, and develop networks. Universities can serve as neutral conveners of these exchanges. Letts, Ryan, and Grossman (1999) also suggest that "professional and education curricula be expanded to help staff succeed . . . in the development of management and organizational process that support effective programs. Much more can be offered about organizational processes aimed at specifically supporting innovation, motivating employees, measuring and improving performance, and so on" (200). The growing number of university degree programs teaching nonprofit management courses (Wish and Mirabella, 1998) can serve as a base for this type of training.

Limited Sharing of Learning

The intermediaries collect an enormous amount of information and are able to train their staff to provide a range of technical assistance. Strategies must be implemented to ensure that the wealth of information and expertise does not stay housed solely within the intermediary but rather that it gets fed back to the staff of the other nonprofits. In other words, we have to find ways to avoid a centralization of skill and knowledge. Following are some preliminary ideas for how an open exchange of information can be created.

1. Funders should provide substantial support to enhance the web sites of the various intermediaries—special emphasis should be given to those intermediaries' web sites that are likely to attract new networks of users. The web sites should provide substantial information, linkages to related web sites, and an interactive space where nonprofits can ask questions and give comments. None of the websites we visited were as sophisticated and attractive as many commercial web sites. Funds should go also go toward advertising the web sites and making them known to diverse networks of nonprofits.

2. Just as important, support needs to go to train nonprofit managers to access and use web sites as effective tools for information. Free workshops offered conveniently—maybe in the nonprofit of-

fices—throughout a city for a two-week period would bring attention to the importance of using web site information.

3. Funders should also give priority to creating exchanges of staff
members between the intermediaries and nonprofits. Paid "fellowships and internships" could be created that provide an opportunity
for senior managers of intermediaries (program directors and the
like) to spend several months in the offices of small and emerging
nonprofits working with teams to complete specific projects—for example, assessing information systems. Rewarding intermediary staff
members for investing time working directly with other nonprofits
would foster a culture of sharing.

4. "Reverse exchanges" can be created for the managers of nonprofits—middle management can spend several months working
on specific projects within intermediaries. Of course, the nonprofits
have to be rewarded or at least compensated for the loss of staff time.
Funders should reward intermediaries who make information readily
available to nonprofits including data collected from nonprofits.

Conclusions

More than ever, senior staff members of nonprofits are expected to
have the skills needed to manage in a complex and changing environment. Doing so effectively requires that these organizations develop
three types of organizational capacity—program delivery, program
expansion, and adaptive capacity. The evidence suggests that intermediaries can play an important role in assisting nonprofits to develop these capacities through technical assistance, targeted training,
provision of access to capital, and by making available relevant policy
and practitioner information. The intermediaries can also continue
to play an active role in advocating and lobbying for changes that
could support the mission of the smaller nonprofits.

The emergence of an *intermediary sub sector* can be hailed as a positive development if the partnership between smaller nonprofits and
the intermediaries is carefully nourished. The absence of strategies to
encourage and facilitate use of intermediaries beyond a narrow circle,
can increasingly position intermediaries as competitors for funds and
not supporters of the nonprofit sector at large. This chapter argues

for implementation of strategies that encourage a strong, supportive partnership.

The partnership between nonprofits and intermediaries can be greatly enhanced by overcoming three major challenges now confronting the field: (1) nonprofits' lack of access to intermediaries; (2) funder ignorance—that is, lack of support for capacity building and open dialogue between intermediaries and smaller nonprofits; and (3) limited sharing of information created by intermediaries.

Potential strategies are suggested for beginning to overcome these challenges and include: (1) expanding the reach of intermediaries—especially the large and well-capitalized ones—to new networks of nonprofits—and increasing culturally sensitive technical assistance and training; (2) association of funders—affinity groups and the like—need to emphasize continuously the importance of funding the development of organizational capacity in the nonprofit sector and (3) staff of nonprofits should have access to the wealth of information created by the major intermediaries through increased attention to the Internet as a vehicle of information exchange and through targeted staff exchanges.

Spending Policies for Foundations

The Case for Increased Grants Payout

PERRY MEHRLING

Spending Policies for Foundations

After 1981, when Congress relaxed payout[1] requirements to a minimum 5% of net investment assets, the ratio of grants payout to assets for the universe of foundations fell precipitously from about 8% in 1981 to about 6% by the end of the decade (see figure 7.1). In recent years, the ratio has declined further, falling below 5% in 1997. Such a low grants payout ratio may still meet the letter of the law because grants are not the only "qualifying distribution" that meets the legal requirement, and because foundations are allowed to average over five years. The question is whether such a low grants payout ratio is now economically sensible.

The aggregate figures on grants payout are subject to the criticism that the universe of foundations is not a homogeneous group. Independent foundations account for the overwhelming majority of total foundation assets and grants. Although this group includes both large and small foundations with rather different payout practices, it is homogeneous in the sense that it is the most prominent group to which the 5% minimum payout requirement applies. Of more concern are the corporate, community, and operating foundations which together account for about 15% of assets and 25% of grants. Does inclusion of these different groups in the aggregate numbers account for the aggregate trend? It is not possible to say for certain, because disaggregated data is available from the Foundation Center only

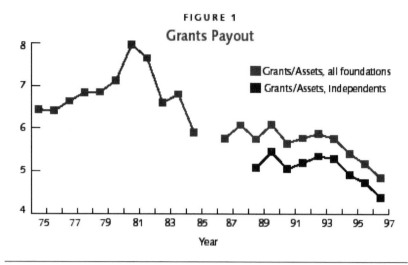

FIGURE 1
Grants Payout

Figure 7.1 Grants Payout
Source: Foundation Center, *Foundation Giving, 1998,* Tables 9 and 10; "Highlights of the
Foundation Center's *Foundation Giving,* 1999 Edition." The Foundation Center provides published
aggregate data on all private foundations back to 1975. Data on independent foundations is
taken from *Foundation Giving,* 1991–1999 editions.

since 1989, but the available data show that grants payout for independent foundations tracks the aggregate numbers fairly closely (see
Figure 7.1).

Table 7.1 allows us to assess the potential bias involved in an aggregative analysis. It is clear that inclusion of corporate and community foundations tends to raise the aggregate grants payout ratio,
because these subcategories have higher grants payout than the independent foundations. Balancing this effect somewhat, inclusion
of operating foundations tends to lower the aggregate grants payout
ratio. Another concern is that changes over time in the relative size
of the different categories, as well as changes over time in the grants
payout ratio within each category, may affect aggregate trends. In
this respect, inclusion of corporate foundations tends to exacerbate
the measured decline in grants payout, since corporate foundations
were relatively larger and had higher grants payout in 1989 than in
1997. Balancing this effect somewhat, inclusion of the community
and operating foundations tend to reduce the measured decline in

Table 7.1   Disaggregation Analysis, Grants Payout Trends, 1989–1997

	Independent	Corporate	Community	Operating	Total
1989 Assets (%)	86.8	4.2	4.4	5.7	100
1997 Assets (%)	86.7	3.3	6.0	5.1	100
1989 Grants (%)	75.7	17.3	5.4	1.6	100
1997 Grants (%)	77.4	13.0	7.5	2.2	100
1989 Grants/Assets (%)	5.08	23.9	7.1	1.6	5.75
1997 Grants/Assets (%)	4.38	19.0	6.1	2.1	4.85

Source: Foundation Center, *Foundation Giving,* 1991–1999 editions.

grants payout. The overall effect can be assessed by comparing the aggregate decline from 5.75% to 4.85% with the decline for independent foundations only from 5.08% to 4.38%. Disaggregation changes absolute magnitudes somewhat, but it does not change the overall trend.

Foundation Growth

Since 1981, foundation assets and grants have grown strongly, both in absolute terms and relative to relevant benchmarks. Figure 7.2 charts that growth by following the ratio of total foundation assets to financial assets of households and nonprofit organizations and the ratio of total grants to gross domestic product. Note that the two series are plotted on different vertical scales. Both series show steady growth since 1981, accelerating somewhat since 1995. Both grants and assets have increased, but assets have increased faster, which accounts for the Ming ratio of grants payout to assets.

It is helpful to put these numbers in longer historical perspective. Nelson (1987, Table 5–2, p. 130) reports comparable figures for the more limited universe of private foundations between 1962 and 1981. Over that period, relative assets fell from 1. 16% to .86%, and relative grants fell from .107% to .087%.[2] Over the same period, the ratio of grants to assets rose from 4.8% to 6.1% (Nelson, Table 5-1, p. 129). This is the context that Congress had in mind in 1981 when

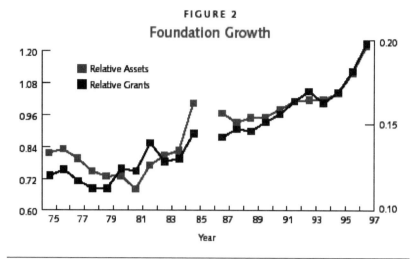

FIGURE 2

Foundation Growth

Figure 7.2 Foundation Growth
Source: Foundation Center, *Foundation Giving,* 1998. Tables 9 and 10; "Highlights of the Foundation Center's *Foundation Giving,* 1999 Edition." Board of Governors of the Federal Reserve, Table B.100 "Balance Sheet of Households and Nonprofit Organizations." *Economic Report of the President 1999,* Table B-1 "Gross domestic product, 1959–98."

it reduced required payout to 5%, a context that is almost exactly opposite the current one.

It is tempting to read the record of the last two decades as a vindication of the lowered payout ratio, but a closer look at the source of asset growth makes clear that the lowered payout ratio had very little to do with it. Table 7.2 shows that almost all of the increase in foundation assets has come from new gifts into new and existing foundations and very little from returns on existing assets in excess of payout. (See footnote 3 for details about how the calculation was done.) New gifts accounted for 84.5% of the increase, while a net increase of existing assets accounted for only 15.5%. Put another way, of the 5.81% average annual real asset growth over this period, fully 4.36% was accounted for by new gifts received and only 1.38% by an increase of existing assets.[3]

Congress intended that the 5% minimum payout requirement would give foundations the opportunity to rebuild, and foundations did so at the rate of 1.38% annually. What Congress did not antici-

Table 7.2   Investment and Gifts, Foundation Growth Rate Components, Total Foundations, 1977–1996

Constant 1975 Dollars, in billions	
1996 assets including those received in 1978–1996	91.75
New gifts received in 1978–1996	50.98
1996 assets excluding those received in 1978–1996	40.77
Increase of 1977 assets net of payout	9.37
1977 assets	31.4
Annual asset growth, 1977–1996	
Total growth	5.81%
Gifts and new foundation formation	4.36%
Investment return net of payout	1.38%

Source: Foundation Giving, 1998. The Foundation Center's figures for gifts received begin only in 1978. Figures for gifts received in 1986 were not available, which biases the figures toward an underestimate of the importance of new gifts received.

pate was that new gifts would be so strong as to swamp the contribution of internal return. Two decades later, it is clear that foundation assets would have grown strongly even if payout had been 1% higher, and this historical pattern appears likely to continue into the foreseeable future.

Perpetuity and Payout

The Individual Foundation

Recognizing that there is no longer a case for keeping payout low in order to rebuild foundation assets, those who favor limiting payout to 5% focus instead on maintaining existing assets whole in the face of uncertain future asset returns. The most prominent such analysis is that of DeMarche Associates (1995). Their analysis differs from the preceding by its focus on the experience of a hypothetical single foundation with a typical asset mix of stocks and bonds instead of on the actual experience of the entire universe of foundations. For the sake of comparison, table 7.3 shows the results of their alternative methodology when applied to the last twenty years.[4] If anything, the

Table 7.3 Summary Analysis of Different Charitable Payout Scenarios, 1975–1994 (in thousands of dollars)

| | Charitable Payout | | | |
	5.0%	6.0%	7.0%	8.0%
1975 Asset Value	1000	1000	1000	1000
1994 Nominal Asset Value	5058	4510	3778	3160
1994 Real Asset Value	1750	1453	1204	996
Average Asset Growth Rate	2.8%	1.9%	.9%	0%
1975 Charitable Payout	50	60	70	80
1994 Charitable Payout	269	271	264	253
1975–1994 Total Payout	2866	3082	3226	3314

Source: DeMarche Associates (1995, Tables 3–5) and author's calculations. All calculations include .5% investment management expense in addition to charitable payout.

results are even more supportive of the conclusion that there is room for increased payout. Even an 8% charitable payout (which is 8.5% total payout allowing .5% for investment expenses) would have maintained the real asset value of the hypothetical foundation's endowment. Note also that the total charitable payout over the twenty-year period would have been higher with 8% payout than with 5%.[5]

It should be noted that the figures in table 7.3 depend on the time period, which was chosen to match as closely as possible the time period for which the aggregative Foundation Center data is available. DeMarche Associates conducted their analysis for the longer period 1950–1994, and found that 5.0% payout results in asset growth of 25.4% over the whole period, which was about .5% annually, so their analysis supports a payout increase of .5%. Craig (1999) conducted a similar analysis for the period 1900–1999 and found that 5% payout resulted in asset growth of 0% (after subtracting .7% for investment expenses). Since there is no particular reason to think that the distant past provides better information about the future than does the recent past, there is no particular reason to prefer their figures over those in table 7.3. The plain fact of the matter is that we don't know what future asset returns are going to be.

What is the right policy for a foundation facing uncertain future asset returns? Modern finance teaches us that the right policy for an individual wealth holder depends on her degree of risk aversion. The

DeMarche and Craig analyses both draw an analogy between the individual wealth holder and the individual foundation. That analogy is arguably strained, however, since it is questionable whether the foundation is or should be a risk averse wealth maximizer. A better analogy is that between a profit-maximizing firm and the foundation.

A foundation is like a firm that mobilizes its assets in order to maximize profit but with profit conceived more broadly. An ordinary firm makes an investment when the expected benefit is greater than the expected cost and, since both these numbers are naturally expressed in monetary units, the required comparison is relatively easy and the decision is straightforward, at least in principle. For a foundation, things are not as easy because the relevant benefits and costs are not always naturally expressed in monetary units, nor can monetary values always be easily deduced. Nevertheless, the principle is clear: Just like a firm, the goal of a foundation should be to make a "difference" (or some other analogue to the private firm's "profit"), not to perpetuate itself as an entity.

In the world of firms and profit, there are checks that prevent firms from losing sight of their legitimate goals, checks such is takeovers and bankruptcies. The only analogous check in the world of foundations is the 5% minimum payout which, as we have seen, is a rather weak check. The analogy with profit-maximizing firms suggests that payout rates should be high enough that foundations are required to attract new funds in order to pursue their missions. Foundations that do not want to become sterile warehouses of wealth should adopt higher payout rates voluntarily.

From this point of view, the methodology employed by DeMarche/ Harrison and applied in table 7.3 is irrelevant since perpetuity in itself is no legitimate goal of a charitable foundation, nor are the conservative spending and investment policies that follow from adoption of such a goal. As used in this study, table 7.3 can be seen as a bridge between the narrow, individual approach used in DeMarche/Harrison and the broader social approach adopted below.

The Foundation Sector

Behind much of the current debate about payout rates one senses a concern not just to ensure that grantmaking capacity doesn't shrink but even more to ensure that grantmaking capacity grows at least at the rate of growth of the economy, if not faster. However compelling today's social problems are, tomorrow's are likely to be just as compelling and are also likely more expensive given the increasing scale of economic activity. From the point of view of an individual foundation with a fixed endowment, it appears that the only thing it can do to prepare for the future is to set aside some of today's investment return, which means keeping total payout below return. This is the point of view that lies behind much of the resistance to higher payout rates.

From a larger point of view, however, growth of grantmaking capacity depends very little on reinvestment of returns from existing assets and much more on new giving to existing foundations and on new giving to form new foundations. The historical facts on this matter (see table 7.2) are incontrovertible. From the point of view of society as a whole, it is not the asset growth of any individual foundation that matters, but rather the asset growth of the entire collection of foundations. From a social point of view, the collection of foundations appears as one large unified foundation whose assets have grown at 5.81% annually over the last twenty years, which is significantly faster than the rate of growth of the economy.

From a social point of view, even the asset growth of the entire collection of foundations underestimates aggregate grantmaking capacity. What matters is the growth of the total quantity of assets devoted to charitable purposes and the income generated by those assets, whether or not those assets currently reside in a foundation endowment and whether or not that income is channeled through a recognized foundation entity. Classification as a charitable foundation is a tax status and nothing more. If tax law were changed to favor segregation of charitable assets into legal entities called foundations, then foundation assets would grow, but that doesn't mean that charitable assets would grow.

To make the point completely clear, it will help to have in mind the difference between two idealized charitable giving systems: an endowment system and a non-endowment system. In an endowment system, foundations own all charitable assets, and all grants are funded from the income on those assets. In a non-endowment system, foundations hold no assets and all grants are funded by new giving that flows into foundations from the income generated by charitable assets held elsewhere. Note that in a non-endowment system, it makes no sense to calculate a payout ratio for an individual foundation, since foundation assets in the denominator of such a ratio are zero. Note further that, though the two systems look very different, total grants will be the same as long as total charitable assets are the same in each system.

Which of these systems best describes the U.S. charitable giving system? The attention paid to payout ratios suggests that people think of the U.S. system as an endowment system, but is it? Not when you take an aggregative point of view. Figure 7.3 shows that over the last two decades new foundation creation and gifts into existing foundations has been approximately the same order of magnitude as total foundation grants. Summing over the period 1978–1996, new gifts received was $50.98 billion (in constant 1975 dollars) while total grants were $57.64 billion. This is the pattern one would expect to observe in a non-endowment system in which all gifts received are spent on current grants. Figure 7.3 shows that, in effect, the entire foundation sector has been behaving as though it were a non-endowment passthrough foundation, spending current giving and leaving existing assets almost untouched.

To the extent that the U.S. charitable system is a non-endowment system, it makes no sense to limit total payout to only 5% of whatever assets happen to be on foundation balance sheets at a moment in

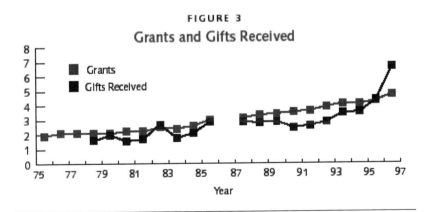

Figure 7.3 Grants and Gifts Received
Source: Foundation Center, *Foundation Giving, 1998,* Tables 9 and 10.

time. Furthermore, and also to the extent that the U.S. charitable system is a non-endowment system, measured payout ratios are much less relevant to the question of perpetuity than is commonly realized.

Conclusion

No one says that individual non-endowment foundations (for example, most corporate foundations), which necessarily have very high payout ratios, are by virtue of their high payout endangering the perpetuation of their charitable mission. The reason no one says this is that it is apparent that there are perfectly adequate assets generating the payout. They just happen to be on the balance sheet of the foundations' sponsors, not of the foundations themselves. By analogy, to the extent that the U.S. foundation sector operates as if it were a non-endowment system, the measured payout ratio has very little to do with the issue of perpetuation of the charitable mission of the foundation sector as a whole.

The impetus for the current discussion about increasing payout (see Odendahl and Feeney 1999 and Craig 1999) is, no doubt, the strength of recent asset returns. From an economic point of view, the true importance of recent asset returns is that they have swelled the volume of charitable assets held outside current foundation management. It is these assets, not the investment return net of payout on existing foundation assets, on which perpetuation of the charitable mission of the foundation sector depends.

Finally, it needs to be remembered that the 5% minimum payout requirement imposed by Congress is there not to keep foundations from paying out too much but to keep them from paying out too little. Putting the point more sharply, Congress intended to keep tax-favored foundations from becoming mere warehouses of wealth. To the extent that the foundation sector operates as though it were a non-endowment system, paying out new giving while allowing existing assets to compound in perpetuity, the foundation sector is in danger of appearing to be exactly what Congress wanted to prevent (and probably still wants to prevent). To the extent that individual foundations reduce payout to the legal minimum simply in order to increase their assets under management, they defeat the real social purpose of their privileged tax status and risk attracting renewed legislative attention.

Part III

Ideas and Information: Power and Access

8

THE DIGITAL DIVIDE

Communities and Technology

TYSHAMMIE COOPER

In every country, certain groups of people have access to the best information and technology. People known as "the haves," possess powerful computers, fast telephone and Internet service, as well as technical training and financial resources. Another group of people, known as "the have-nots," lack access to new or good computers and reliable telephone and Internet services. This disparity in access to technology, information, training, and financial resources between these two groups of people is called the digital divide. There has always been a gap in communities where some people can make effective use of information technology and others who cannot. Now, more than ever, unequal access to technology excludes many people from reaping the fruits of the twenty-first century. We use the term "digital divide" to refer to the gap between those who can use new information and communication tools effectively, to improve their lives and those who cannot or lack access.

During the Clinton administration, extensive research of the digital divide was conducted to review its effects on American communities. The *Falling Through the Net: Toward Digital Inclusion* report, published by the Commerce Department in October 2000, concluded that more than half of all households have computers and that more than half of all Americans will be using the Internet by the middle of 2001. While the digital divide has decreased in some cases, it slightly expanded in others, although Internet access and computer ownership rose rapidly for all ethnic groups.

Some studies reveal that all users, regardless of class, gender, or race, face two major barriers: the cost and difficulty of Internet research and use. The most severely affected groups are the poor, elderly, certain minority groups (African and Hispanic Americans), and the physically challenged. As demonstrated in the most recent data, large gaps remain between black and Hispanic households that have computers and Internet access when measured against the national average Internet penetration rate (blacks: 23.5% , Hispanics: 23.6%, national: 41.5%).

While much of the public's concern about the digital divide has focused on the gap between haves and have-nots (the differences among the races), a new dimension of the digital divide is shaping up. This new dimension has a profound impact on young people, the unemployment rate, and business. High-tech companies of California's Silicon Valley cannot find enough computer-literate workers, a shortage that is costing them more than $3 billion per year. Poor neighborhoods were always a part of Silicon Valley and light years away from the high-tech companies. These companies are now turning to these neighborhoods to train workers. The inability of low-income Americans to access computers and the Internet has shut them out of opportunity in several important ways. First, more companies are starting to advertise job announcements via the Internet and, second, many government agencies have created web sites to disseminate information, update personal information, and receive government benefits. Neither of these are an option if one does not possess resources.

The Digital Divide Progress

Today in the twenty-first century, everything is computerized. A simple shopping trip to the grocery store or the mall, involves computers. From touch screen computers, to talking ATMs, to online bill payment, to signing up for disability or unemployment benefits, success depends upon your ability to use computers and understand technology. As a result of the obvious need to close this gap, the federal government and private corporations have allocated millions of dollars toward digital divide initiatives, which have been called, "bridging the divide."

Numerous programs around the nation during the mid-1990s were developed as a result. Many private corporations as well as the federal government established digital divide grants and other programs to provide non-profit and other community-based organizations with financing and computer equipment essential to bridge the divide in their communities. Comcast Cable Communications, AOL Time Warner, Gateway, and Microsoft, to name a few, are some of the companies that have launched philanthropic ventures, public service announcements, request for proposals (RFPs), and/or offered discounts to people who donated old computers[1] in order to promote the importance of computer literacy among communities affected by the digital divide.

There has been an enormous change between the haves and the have-nots in the digital divide. Overall computer ownership has steadily grown from 10 to 13 percent since 1994. In 1999, the number of African American households online grew by 44 percent. In 2001, more than half of the U.S. adult population ventured online within the first six months and nearly three-quarters of children ages 12 to 17 had Internet access. Computer costs no longer appears to be a significant factor with most families; however, those living in urban and rural communities still cannot afford them, making non-profit, government agencies, private corporations, and colleges/universities instrumental in implementing digital divide programs. Internet programs, self-sufficiency programs, and other programs have used aggressive initiatives, strategies, and benchmarks to reduce numbers, reach their targeted audiences, and bridge the gap through computer and job training. They often become recognized as best practices programs.

Some of the projects that have been recognized as best practices programs are Plugged In, a program in East Palo Alto, California, the University of Washington–Digital Divide Project, PowerUp, a consortium of non-profit, private corporations, that developed a national initiative to bring computers and the Internet to children in poor communities and Community Technology Centers' Network (CTCNet), is a network of more than three hundred community technology centers that provide computer access to people in low-income communities.

The common goal of the best practices programs is educating people about the divide, providing computer and Internet access, and software training. An effective program integrates the needs of the community and the population to program services. To develop a digital divide best practices model, the program should have a clearly targeted audience, objectives, and effective marketing. It should also have an ongoing feedback mechanism from the clients served and a thorough evaluation plan to review the effectiveness of the program in decreasing the divide.

Developing a Best Practices Model

Planning

Whether it's developing your mission statement, creating a class curriculum, or writing a grant effectively, thorough planning will assist in mapping out an overview of the program. Also during this phase, you research various funding opportunities. The goals and objectives are developed during this first phase and serve as the road map that helps to identify the purpose of the program, accomplishments to be made, and the potential client base in the community served.

Objectives

During this phase, specific goals and plans to accomplish them in relation to the overall plan continue to be developed. The targeted audience defines the skill level and curriculum structure that is designed with the aid of a program outline. The curriculum should include lessons such as understanding how a computer works, software applications, benefits of learning new technology and how these lessons can make a person more marketable. It is crucial that the program not only teaches technology, but also emphasizes the benefits.

Effective Marketing

After you identify your audience, you have to develop a way to reach them. The marketing plan has to be persuasive because the targeted audience will be doubtful about how this program will be life-changing. The message has to be appropriate for audiences, and it has to explain clearly the benefits of the program. Audience background will help guide marketing efforts. Marketing materials should be created while remembering that the press may review communications.

Evaluation

This component is always overlooked, but it is highly regarded by funders. Evaluation demonstrates program effectiveness and changes in demographic information. It may be relevant to funders who need to know a lot of information about the program.

Funding

Creating a best practices program can sometimes be a strenuous process. However, if you follow some of the tips above, they will serve as tools to bridge the divide when creating a program. The tips will help you get started on a road to success because you will be on a path to creating a professional, comprehensive, and solid program that you can submit for funding. Good planning, a strong marketing campaign, and an effective evaluation process will assist in securing financial contributions. No matter how great or well planned the message is, nothing gets done without resources.

There are many programs that give away the tools of technology, in an age when wealth built on technology has spurred significant growth in philanthropy. Although billions of dollars have been spent or set aside for this endeavor, not all initiatives have been fruitful. With each passing year, being connected and being computer literate becomes more critical in achieving economic and educational advancement. That's why it is important that we move as quickly as possible toward digital inclusion.

Shortcomings of the Digital Divide: What Happened?

The digital divide may be decreasing, but still there is a desperate need for additional computers and education in non-profit organizations and low-income communities. Many community-based programs have been unsuccessful because residents were unable to see the direct benefits of the program and therefore not willing to participate. A program participant in Silicon Valley, stated, "She was afraid about joining the program because she didn't know what she was going to get out of it and there are many others like her."

A lack of education is also a serious problem. If one can't read and write, one will have difficulties learning how to operate a computer. Many young members of communities are computer illiterate because their schools cannot offer adequate services. Does billions of dollars fill the gap in digital divide computer programs lead to fewer teachers, books, and libraries, less teacher training, larger classes, and fewer athletic, lunch, music, art, and recreation programs?

While most large corporations are racing to keep up with the perpetual changes of technology, many smaller non-profit organizations and churches are barely out of the starting block. There are many churches and community organizations that don't have money to purchase computers to allow them or their members access to the Internet. This is very alarming because non-profit organizations and churches are in an important position to help shift and shape the dialogue around the digital divide and create solutions for narrowing the technology and communications gap in rural and urban America. In these communities, non-profits and churches often serve those most affected by the divide, but many find that the challenges facing their clients are often the same that face the organizations themselves. Communications tools, that is, computers, Internet access, modems, and telephones have a great potential to aid non-profits in bridging the social divide in this country, but without access to resources, fulfilling this role may prove difficult.

Some companies have launched huge campaigns advertising their efforts to bridge the divide, but many have questioned the motives. The overwhelming response can be traced back to February 2000, when President Clinton announced that his fiscal 2001 budget would include $2 billion in tax incentives over ten years to encourage private sector investment. Many feared the investments were linked to tax deductions and long-term business benefits, rather than corporate social responsibility. Some of the efforts had hidden padding and free marketing. Although it gave some school districts free equipment and Internet access, the teachers and administrators were bombarded with advertisements each time they accessed the Internet. In other cases, companies announced $1 million allotments for digital divide programs, but the funds were split among cities, making the average grant amount between $50,000 to $100,000. The result of this was that this wasn't enough money to address the needs of thousands of people.

Critics also felt that another motive driving corporate America was the computer companies' direct stake in addicting kids to computers and emphasizing machines over teachers to increase sales. Whether altruistic or motivated by tax breaks, corporate America appears to be working toward closing the divide. Hundreds of companies and the government have invested millions of dollars into programs they say will address the problem. So, while President Clinton felt that "everybody ought to have access to a computer and the Internet," corporate America may not be effective in bridging the Digital Divide.

Is This Reality?

There has always been a gap between the rich and poor. Advances in technology for communications and research has broadened this gap. Learning how to use computers and the Internet increasingly is becoming crucial to academic and job success. "The difference between students who are successful and those who aren't isn't a matter of how smart they are," said Ms. McClendon, a teacher in the Seattle School District. "Increasingly, it's a matter of how fast they can get the information they need and how that information is used." She says that she is looking forward to this fall, presumably because she is scheduled to receive thirty Internet-ready computers.

Many students learn in Internet and computerized classrooms and go then go home to no technology and parents who are not computer literate. Academics like McClendon fear that the nation's poorest and most poorly educated students are being left behind by a world that is going online at breakneck speed because of the disparity between class and home access.

Money and race are also factors in the digital divide. Although computer prices have fallen below $500, families that struggle to pay bills still cannot afford to purchase computers or pay a $20 monthly fee for Internet access. According to the 2000 Digital Economy report, 87 percent of the 5.5 million white, Asian and Pacific Islander families living in urban areas and headed by someone with at least a college education had home computers, and 68 percent had Internet connections. Black and Hispanic households with similar circumstances are as likely to have computers, but they are 14 percent less likely to have Internet access at home. In addition to money and race factors, the higher your education level, the more likely you are to own a computer.

Other proponents of the digital divide have argued that the initiatives have fallen short because many ethnic groups don't find the content to be of interest to them. Charles Ellison, co-founder of www.politicallyblack.com, argues "drawing minorities to the Web is as much about good content as anything."

Politicians and the media contend capitalism will fix the digital divide problems because computer and Internet cost have dropped to affordable levels. Computer prices have fallen 12 percent between 1987 and 1994 and 26 percent from 1995 to 1999, according to the Digital Economy 2000 report. Although politicians are optimistic about the digital divide for everyday Americans, they do not fully understand how the digital divide affects politics.

While the technology era was well under way, former President Clinton was spear-heading initiatives to close the digital divide between the rich and the poor and former Vice President Al Gore coined the phrase "information superhighway." Although Clinton and Gore developed many efforts to close the divide, Republicans surged ahead of Democrats in technology. It took the 2000 elections for Democrats to comprehend that they had to get on board with the technological revolution. "Technology could have helped us prevent a Florida," says Terry McAuliffe, chairman of the Democratic National Committee. "We would have been able to mobilize more voters to go to the polls." The Florida GOP sent close to 10,000 e-mails during the 2000 elections in Florida to motivate people to vote. Gore lost the state—and the presidency—by 537 votes.

When McAuliffe took over the Democratic Party, the Republicans e-mail list contained of over 1 million activists compared to the Democrats 70,000. In addition to being another source of communication, technology is welcoming to Democrats because they perpetually raise less money than Republicans. "It costs close to 50 cents" to send ordinary mail, McAuliffe says, "it costs no money to e-mail."

In 2000, the Internet made a permanent mark in politics because it provided new avenues for politicians to recruit volunteers and to raise money quickly. The question of how well it is working has yet to be answered, but both sides definitely have witnessed an impact. In 2000 alone, Democrats won a Senate seat by 2,229 votes and two House Republicans won by 111 and 115 votes.

Today, the GOP has 1.7 million names and Democrats have 300,000. Both parties have created web sites for you to log onto— "tell a friend," "review platforms," or "send a link"—to find information on their parties events and elected officials and campaign news.

Although Democrats have somewhat decreased the divide for their party and the voters, they are still lagging behind like other Americans possibly due to financial resources.

Digital Divide: Future Opportunities

The growth of the Internet's use is not surprising considering twenty-seven years ago there were only 50,000 computers. Now over 50,000 computers are sold per day. That's about 20 million PCs per year. One-third of all homes in America have PCs and out of those, 40 percent have modems; 60 percent have CD ROM drives. About 20 million homes have multimedia capability. The Internet now serves 15 million in fifty countries, and usage is growing at 15 percent a month. Current consumers are surrounded constantly by computer technology. They complete financial transactions online, at ATMs, and over the telephone, not with tellers in branch office. Computers and the Internet are now used to locate hotels, restaurants, and complete travel arrangement. Years ago computer phobia was widespread; today it's cool and hip.

Today's youth no longer read newspapers, but access them online. Youth are able to learn about different countries and cultures worldwide with the invention of the Internet. Students can conduct research for papers from home, make informed presentations, complete exams quicker, and the information is more up-to-date, unlike the old-fashioned way of research in the library. With e-mail, they can contact sources to ask questions and perform interviews for more detailed information.

Consumer trust of the Internet has increased. Secure transactions via the Internet have increased. People purchase products, upload personal information, and conduct business online. The Internet has quickly become a major player in our economy. Future developers, consumers, and businesses affected by these trends must take into consideration the people negatively affected by the digital divide.

Seattle, Washington, and Mendocino, California, provide glimpses of effective programs at work. Students in Seattle have e-mail accounts, which they can call up using hundreds of public computer terminals. A small but growing number of computers open to the public offer the latest in multimedia technology. In the Mendocino Unified School District, middle school students are learning the mathematics of linear and exponential growth via satellite uplinks. Students go to computers and venture out using the Internet, where they download geography, math, and computer science programs to assist in their homework and lessons. "Telecommunications . . . will only increase students' interest in these projects, as well as help them get ready for the use of this powerful tool in the real world," says Joan Carlson, the math teacher who designed the project. The marriage of computers and the Internet has created unimagined opportunities for students to reach beyond their classroom walls and become engaged in challenging, real-world tasks.

America is moving rapidly to connect classrooms to advanced communications networks. AOL Time Warner's grant program is the latest in a series of philanthropic activities. The company launched AOL@SCHOOL, a program that provides schools with free access to the Internet. The program offers age-specific content for elementary, middle, and high school students, and special safety tools so teachers and students can access educational web sites easily. Although teachers' areas feature ads, students only see the AOL logo and cannot connect to shopping or pornography sites. However, they will be able to utilize chat rooms and instant messaging at the school's discretion.

With continued support from companies like AOL Time Warner, about 95 percent of schools are connected to the Internet. Wired students are provided online encyclopedias, dictionaries, homework assistance, and college and career preparation. Students can check homework assignments, read news, and send questions to their teachers and classmates, all within a protected environment. Teachers and parents also are able to access online lesson plans, teaching materials, articles, and other useful information.

Students all over America and the rest of the world are using the Internet to learn how to research and analyze information to solve problems and to better communicate. But this potential cannot be tapped fully unless everyone has some kind of access to a computer and technology. Additional steps must be taken to ensure that this investment is worthwhile by:

- Involving parents their children's schooling
- Restructuring schools and non-profit organizations to become catalysts for bringing advanced communication services to their communities
- Changing the roles of teachers from preparing students to pass a test to teaching them to becoming proactive thinkers and learners

Advocacy organizations find the Internet to be effective in communicating about issues, educating the public, and inspiring people to act on issues. In this time of competing demands for resources, some non-profits are discovering the value (and challenges) of forming partnerships to advance their missions. Fund raising, grant writing, marketing, and research for non-profits have changed with technological advances. By partnering with dot-com companies, fund raising, empowering communities, marketing, and bridging the divide, have been taken to the next level. Internet users can even make donations and get involved with some of their favorite charities online. Dave Evenson who is the vice president of Donor-Net said, "The internet will maximize our exposure so that surfers can easily locate the charity they want to support and make a secured donation online."

Conclusion

In a February 2001 *New York Times* article, Federal Communications Commission Chairman Michael Powell said, the phrase "digital divide" is a description of the existing gaps in access to information services and technologies. After expressing commitment to "eliminate barriers," he responded to reporters' questions concerning the divide.

"I think there is a 'Mercedes divide,'" he said. "'I'd like to have one; I can't afford one.' I'm not meaning to be completely flip about this. I think it's an important social issue. But it shouldn't be used to justify the notion of essentially the socialization of the deployment of the infrastructure." It is agreed that no one should be entitled to things, for example—Mercedes cars, just because they live in America. However, the digital divide is not about things you purchase after you earn wealth or status, it's about information, exchange of that information, access, and the impact it has on people that are left out.

The digital divide is often attributed to race, but income appears to be the predominant factor that determines whether people have computers or are online. Extensive gaps continue to exist between ethnic groups, but the largest gap lies between families with high and low incomes, according to "Assessing the Digital Divide(s)." Households with incomes of more than $75,000 make up the largest group of web surfers. That figure will grow to 20 million in 2005. Households with incomes of less than $15,000 will represent only 3 million online households this year and 9 million by 2005.

As computers become increasingly important to economic and social success, many people in inner cities and rural areas are failing to acquire technology as rapidly as their affluent counterparts because they are unaware of the benefits or they cannot afford to make this purchase. Government policies and corporate initiatives are needed to ensure information gaps or socioeconomic statuses do not widen the divide.

Over the years, attention to the digital divide has increased. Despite press coverage, public debates, summits, conferences, and articles, no one has offered the context or perspective that is needed to understand what's at stake and how to ease the problem. Putting predictions and opinions aside, the truth is, technology is continuously changing. It has become a permanent part of the future and society, and it's up for grabs. We still have an opportunity to set expectations. It's the opportunity to make sure that the media, businesses, and government recognize our roles not only as consumers, but also as citizens.

A long time ago, it was established that certain communication tools are so fundamental that the marketplace alone shouldn't determine their provisions and access. It was the dawn of the "Digital

Age," and steps must be taken to ensure the necessary technology will be set at an affordable price. The technology will take the shape of the manufacturers that design it, but the consumers that buy it and the policymakers that set the rules to govern it will define the boundaries.

The Internet coupled with technology that is continuously changing has made a fundamental impact on the way we do business because it has produced one of the greatest periods of wealth in history and the way we deliver and receive information around the world. Throughout the world, countries have been affected by the technological revolution, and the impact is great because 80 percent of the world's inhabitants have never heard a dial tone or seen a computer.

Equal access to basic information and communication tools shapes people's ability to manage day to day. At the same time, society is affected since the value and effectiveness of any system depends on people having access to it. At stake is whether individuals can participate fully in today's job market and whether underserved communities can obtain the tools to flourish and become empowered. Ensuring society benefits from contributions that make our communities diverse, is the very fiber that makes our economy and culture attractive to others.

While there is no consensus on the extent of the divide and whether it's growing or narrowing, some people unanimously acknowledge that some divide exists. This is only the beginning; the Internet is here, and it will remain an integral key to succeeding in our economy.

9

THE MEDIA AND SOCIAL RESPONSIBILITY

Building Public Will for Change

HEATHER BENT TAMIR

Social change activists are becoming increasingly aware of the role that media organizations play in shaping public agendas. Media organizations that provide news coverage, in particular, have the power to influence public debate about crucial social issues. Activists increasingly realize that media strategies are central to social change efforts. With the proliferation of cable news channels, newsmagazine shows, and online and ethnic media outlets, advocates have more opportunities than ever to get their message out. By working with the media, they seek to deepen public understanding about issues that continue to limit opportunity in America, to change public perceptions, and, ultimately, to influence the policy environment.

While most social change organizations recognize the importance of becoming media savvy, many do not have the built-in capacity to develop media contacts. Some rely on public relations firms to assist them, committing themselves to social change work; others depend on organizations that specialize in media training. Fortunately, funders of these organizations are beginning to acknowledge communications as an integral part of grant-making strategy and, as a result, more organizations are developing their own media expertise.

As a social change organization founded in 1999, PolicyLink seeks to achieve fair and equitable policies for low-income communities of color that provide for full inclusion and broad economic participation in American life. The focus of its work is on advancing community-oriented solutions that achieve economic and social equity.

From its inception, PolicyLink recognized communications as a central functional component, the others being research and policy development, and civic engagement and capacity building. To underscore how serious the organization regarded communications, it located its communications arm in New York City—the media capital of the world—while the corporate headquarters is based in Oakland, California. The office would be run by a seasoned director with a staff of experienced professionals. The PolicyLink decision signaled a new level of commitment to communications that is rare in the social change arena and solidified the organization's image as sophisticated, media-savvy, and goal-oriented.

This chapter examines several key accomplishments that PolicyLink has achieved in working with the media to deepen public debate about critical issues and to influence public will. It explores the strategies that this new nonprofit is using and the issues it is addressing. It points to some of the lessons learned about the media's responsibilities and sheds light on the opportunities that exist for social change organizations in a challenging media environment.

Telling the Story of Change Through the Media

PolicyLink is interested in telling the stories about what works to solve the nation's problems. A whole new generation of approaches has emerged that advance opportunity and inclusion but are not widely known. PolicyLink endeavors to shine a light on them and spread the word that solutions exist, hoping to build the public will and public commitment for change that can have an impact in the policy arena.

The communications efforts of PolicyLink go hand in hand with its research and policy development, and capacity building and civic engagement work. With its partners, the organization identifies and develops promising approaches and practices that advance equity and foster a different kind of thinking. These approaches and practices are often documented in research publications and are disseminated widely. The capacity building and civic engagement arm

enables PolicyLink to interact with local constituencies as partners on the ground, testing new ideas and solutions and informing policy. Through this network, PolicyLink—though a national
organization—is connected to local initiatives and to the stories that
can be lifted for national dialogue.

The Social Justice Agenda

Due to the terrorist attacks on September 11, social change
organizations—already fighting an uphill battle in trying to advance
a domestic agenda—now face an even more difficult challenge: refo-
cusing the news media's attention on social justice issues. The media's
near-total preoccupation with the tragic events of that day, and the
aftermath, combined with an outburst of patriotic spirit, have swept
many issues under the rug. America's simmering racial and ethnic
tensions have for the moment subsided, and policemen, long feared
and resented in communities of color, have become overnight heroes.
Social friction caused by issues such as gentrification have eased
substantially. Racial profiling has become an issue that Americans of
Middle Eastern descent must now deal with, removing the spotlight,
but not the reality, from African Americans (Sengupta, 2001).

The social justice agenda, however, remains compelling and urgent,
in some ways even more so since the terrorist attacks. Many low-
income people, employed in the service sector, have lost or are in danger of losing their jobs. The shock to the country's economic system
has left those at the bottom extremely vulnerable, highlighting the
need for a better safety net. In spite of the show of national unity, real
inclusion has yet to be achieved. Many people of color continue to be
shut out of the economic and social mainstream for a variety of reasons, whether due to geographic isolation, low-paying jobs, or lack of
financial assets. The country still needs policies and strategies that enable all racial groups to prosper and to have access to opportunity.

PolicyLink seeks to fulfill this need by building public support for
strategies that work. In spite of an inhospitable media climate, the
organization has achieved some encouraging results. One of its earli-
est communications efforts involved working with supporters of the
Community Reinvestment Act (CRA)—a law that requires banks to

provide loans in their service areas and that was under attack in Congress—to preserve key components of the act that provided benefits to low-income communities. PolicyLink worked with community groups on the ground to frame their messages, launched targeted media campaigns in key congressional districts, and sought to tell the stories of how the CRA had helped to revitalize communities. In the end, Congress passed new regulations in November 1999 that preserved most of the components that community activists had campaigned for.

PolicyLink has continued to build on its CRA activities, working to bring attention to strategies that help achieve inclusion and social justice. It is now focused on promoting solutions to other issues that contribute to inequity, such as urban disinvestment and suburban sprawl, the widening wealth gap, the digital divide, and the prevalence of police abuse and misconduct in low-income communities of color.

The Challenges

The PolicyLink focus on solutions is at odds with a media environment that plays up negativity and sensationalism in a quest for big ratings and profits. That negative climate is broadbased and acknowledged throughout the industry. For example, in an August 9, 2001, interview on *The Today Show*, veteran broadcast journalist Walter Cronkite agreed that the news business had become "skewed toward the more sensational. The profession of journalism ought to be about telling people what they need to know, not what they want to know." Don Hewitt, originator and longtime producer of *60 Minutes*, in reflecting on the state of the industry in his new memoir *Tell Me A Story*, admitted that "journalists have enormous power" and that "too often we take the low road" (Hewitt, 2001: 230).

Evidence of the irresponsibility of the news media can be found in the sometimes overblown treatment that crime stories receive. A survey released by Building Blocks for Youth (Dorfman and Schiraldi, 2001) found that between 1990 and 1998, network news coverage of homicides increased 473 percent while homicides actually decreased nearly 33 percent during that same period. The report also found that at a time of declining crime rates among youth of color, the news media overemphasized crimes committed by these youth, leading to a heightened perception of their role in criminal acts and reinforcing racial stereotypes.

Contributing to these misperceptions is the paucity of people of color in major decision-making roles throughout the news industry. Although some progress has been made, the industry as a whole continues to lack the sensitivity it needs to report adequately on racial issues. A renewed commitment is required to diversify newsrooms and the stories that are covered, and reporters of all ethnicities need to develop the expertise to cover racial issues, creating an atmosphere of inclusion in the newsroom. Realizing that it would not achieve its goal of having the racial balance in newsrooms match the racial balance in the country by the year 2000, the American Society of Newspaper Editors (ASNE) retreated from that goal, instead giving itself until 2025 to achieve that objective. Newspaper newsrooms are now 12 percent minority while the nation is 28 percent minority (Newkirk, 2000). While numbers alone do not tell the whole story, many argue that improving the numbers would improve the overall quality of coverage.

Another criticism leveled at the media is the industry's trend toward conglomeration and merger, oftentimes resulting in staff cuts that affect the quality of news coverage and reducing the probability of new voices being heard. Ethnic news media, long an alternative voice to mainstream outlets, are also merger targets of mainstream media groups, as witnessed by NBC's recent purchase of the Telemundo Communications Group, the nation's second-largest Spanish-language broadcaster, with a 20 percent share of the market (Sorkin, 2001).

Positive Trends

The good news is that journalists themselves increasingly are concerned about some of the negative practices in their industry. Some are seeking to reclaim the high ground and raise journalistic standards through efforts such as the Project for Excellence in Journalism, funded by the Pew Charitable Trusts and based at Columbia

University. In its report, *Framing the News: The Triggers, Frames, and Messages in Newspaper Coverage*, published in 1999, the Project for Excellence sought to identify the narrative frames that journalists use to tell stories as a way to uncover major biases that might exist in newsreporting. *Framing the News* found that there is a "decided tendency" in the press "to present the news through a combative lens." The report also found that newspapers do not do as good a job of explaining and interpreting information and placing issues into larger social and historical contexts, as may be believed. The report confirmed "a presumption on the part of journalists that readers don't care about policy or its impact," with policy stories accounting for "only 8 percent" of stories on the front page of the seven newspapers surveyed (see http://www.journalism.org/publ_research/framing.html).

In other developments, a survey of newspeople conducted between November 1998 and February 1999 by the Pew Research Center for the People and the Press in association with the Committee of Concerned Journalists (an initiative of the Project for Excellence) found that a growing number of journalists, particularly those working at the network level, are bothered by the profit-driven mindset of the news managers and executives to the extent that it hurts or inhibits quality news coverage. In addition, the rate of news media executives and journalists who say lack of credibility with the public is a major reason for declining audiences has risen to one-half of them, up from one-third in 1989, and two-thirds of those in both national and local news agreed that news organizations have moved toward "infotainment" to attract more readers or viewers (The Pew Research Center for the People & the Press, 1999).

Furthermore, for nearly a decade now, a movement known as civic journalism has been trying to influence the practices of mainstream journalism and a new survey seems to indicate that it has contributed to a "sea change" in attitudes and practices in the news business.

The survey, released in the summer of 2001 and sponsored by The Pew Center for Civic Journalism, the Associated Press Managing Editors, and the National Conference of Editorial Writers, finds "a sharply increased appetite for more two-way connections with readers," especially given the advent of new communications technologies. In addition, "more than half" the editors in the survey said they had made a "conscious effort to move away from building their stories around a conventional frame of conflict," and "eight in 10" said "they offer stories about potential solutions to community problems at least some of the time." The survey confirmed that editors are trying to diversify the "voices" in their stories through the development of new source lists and expanded community contacts. Results of the survey are based on responses from 512 U.S. dailies with circulations of 20,000 or more (The Pew Center for Civic Journalism, 2001).

As part of the changing climate, the *Columbia Journalism Review (CJR)* has also identified a growing interest in solutions-oriented stories. Instead of emphasizing only the negatives, more journalists are now interested in also identifying solutions to problems. The *CJR* article noted that the trend cuts across different types of media, including the *New York Times Magazine*, *World News Tonight with Peter Jennings*, *The Nation*, *U.S. News and World Report*, and the *San Diego Union-Tribune*. According to *CJR*, reporters shy away from "solutions" stories because they are more difficult to do and can seem too "saccharin" if not presented with complexity and nuance. The public affairs department of ABC News has stated that it decided to suspend its Solutions series that ran two to three times a week—from August 1996 to September 1997—in part because of the difficulty in finding high-quality stories. Still, others have persevered. Both the *San Diego Union Tribune* and *The Nation*, for example, continue to run regular solutions-oriented pieces, and a newswire service, the American News Service based in Brattleboro, Vermont, focuses exclusively on solutions-oriented stories (Benesch, 1998).

Civic journalism—described by the Pew Center web site as both a philosophy and a set of values with a core belief "that journalism has an obligation to public life," and that it can help "empower a community or it can help disable it" (see http://www.pewcenter.org/doingcj/)—has its detractors, however. MSNBC news anchor Brian Williams maintains that journalists should report problems, not try to solve them, noting "there are other people who have that job" (The Pew Center for Civic Journalism, 2000).

Doing the Work

While opportunities exist, it is clear that challenges remain. The efforts of the PolicyLink communications office to market the organization as a new voice offering a fresh approach in considering the nation's challenges and as a source journalists go to for solutions and analysis are hampered by the climate of negativity and sensationalism that persists. Still, PolicyLink has been able to achieve some positive media results. We now turn to examining how this has been accomplished by exploring two areas of work in greater depth: equitable development and community-centered policing.

Equitable development   From its inception, PolicyLink was concerned about the disconnect between struggling inner cities and affluent surrounding suburbs and saw the country's sprawling residential patterns as a major reason for continuing inequity. It supported the view that the destinies of cities and suburbs are linked and that solutions must be found that allow both to prosper. It began to publicize positive models of communities working to achieve these regional solutions in publications such as *Community Based Initiatives Promoting Regional Equity* (2000) and *Opportunities for Smarter Growth: Social Equity and the Smart Growth Movement*, a joint publication of PolicyLink and the Funders Network for Smart Growth and Livable Communities (1999).

With mounting concern about gentrification and the resulting displacement of low-income residents, PolicyLink saw an opportunity to sharpen its framework and has shaped and advanced equitable development as a solution to urban disinvestment and suburban sprawl. Equitable development promotes tools and strategies that benefit low-income residents of color, whether focusing on affordable housing, job creation, wealth-building, or residents' participation in land use decisions. It seeks to guide public and private investment toward inclusive and beneficial outcomes for low-income people in inner cities and emphasizes the positive aspects of mixed-income communities, recognizing that low-income residents of a metropolitan region are often the least likely to benefit from the economic vitality of that region and yet have the most to gain.

In response to the need in communities, PolicyLink developed and launched on its web site a toolkit to help local communities apply equitable development strategies. Known as the *Equitable Development Toolkit: Beyond Gentrification*, the product was launched (under a different name) in April 2001 and identifies seventy policies and strategies that community leaders can pursue to direct new investments to the benefit of current residents. PolicyLink anticipates developing half of these strategies into full online tools and policy briefs by the end of 2001.

PolicyLink is finding the American people hungry to discuss solutions to issues such as affordable housing and the urban disinvestment that results from sprawl. The public's growing awareness is reflected in the smart growth debate, in the increasing number of coalitions forming across the urban-suburban divide to tackle common problems, and in surveys done by groups such as Smart Growth America that show public support for strategies designed to revitalize urban areas.

Sensing an opportunity to deepen public knowledge about these issues and build public will for policy solutions, PolicyLink began identifying the journalists who were writing about these issues, cultivating media relationships, and developing a media database. It also began placing Letters to the Editor in influential media outlets, such as the *American Prospect*, the *New York Times*, and the *Wall Street Journal*, promoting solutions to urban disinvestment and displacement. As a result of the groundwork it had laid, journalists began identifying PolicyLink as a resource on the issue, and, in April 2001, PolicyLink president Angela Glover Blackwell authored an opinion editorial that appeared in the *New York Times*, building on a series about gentrification in Harlem that had run in the *Times* (see Blackwell, 2001). The Op-ed piece focused on solutions and strategies that community activists and developers can use.

The *New York Times* article gave PolicyLink added momentum; shortly after it was published, the president of PolicyLink was invited to appear on *Nightline*, again focusing on solutions to displacement, this time in a black neighborhood in Atlanta. Recognizing the magnitude of the opportunity and wanting to make the most of it, the communications office took the time to prepare Blackwell for a solutions-oriented discussion. It did not matter that she had previous media experience. Part of doing the work is being able to anticipate questions that may be asked and staying focused and on point. The staff coached Blackwell in media techniques, ran through practice sessions with her, and armed her with examples to use of equitable development strategies that were working on the ground, drawing from the toolkit.

PolicyLink built on these successes; a PolicyLink staff member authored a cover story promoting the tools and strategies of equitable development that appeared in the May/June 2001 issue of *Shelterforce*, a magazine that covers affordable housing issues.

The organization continues to develop and seize opportunities to promote equitable development. It planned targeted media campaigns at the local level to publicize the existence of the toolkit and the solutions that were being advanced. It also had an opportunity to attract additional publicity through the launch of a report, *Sharing the Wealth: Resident Ownership Mechanisms*, growing out of its equitable development work, that examined wealth-building strategies.

Community-centered Policing PolicyLink is having incremental success promoting the notion of community-centered policing. "Community-centered policing" is the PolicyLink term to describe policing practices that involve communities working collaboratively with law enforcement to achieve greater accountability and meaningful change and reform, thus improving community/police relations. Too often, policing is something done to communities, not with communities, and is characterized in low-income communities of color by police misconduct, the use of excessive force, and racial profiling, all practices that erode community confidence and instill fear. Promising community-centered policing practices shows that change is not only necessary, but possible, when police and communities work together.

PolicyLink sought to disseminate information and build public awareness about community-centered policing practices through *Community-Centered Policing: A Force For Change*, released in May 2001. The culmination of a yearlong research effort, *Community-Centered Policing* was completed in partnership with the Advancement Project, a national advocacy group based in Washington, D.C. The report highlights promising policing practices in more than fifty cities, with sections on neighborhood problem-solving, community-conscious personnel policies, community oversight, and collaborative information-gathering and sharing. This area of PolicyLink work recognizes that police misconduct aimed at residents of low-income communities is yet another part of the equation that creates inequitable economic and social outcomes for people of color. It also grows out of the desire to support comprehensive solutions to inequity through shared problem-solving and civic participation.

The PolicyLink communications office developed a national and local media strategy to support the launch of *Community-Centered Policing*, with targeted outreach to broadcast, print, cable, web-based, and ethnic media. Message development focused on the fact that effective partnerships between communities and police departments are attainable, and there are innovative and new models and approaches currently in use that are proven to strengthen community/police relations.

The office also prepared PolicyLink staff to be media spokespeople on the issue, providing training on how to stay on point in media interviews and focused on solutions. The training paid off in several articles in local newspapers across the country, particularly in Cincinatti where PolicyLink had been invited by a local coalition to help organize a meeting on promising policing approaches at a time when the city was reeling from a case of police brutality. Only a few months earlier, a young unarmed black man had been shot to death by a police officer.

PolicyLink worked hard to get positive coverage in Cincinatti and invited news organizations to the convening. In the end, its efforts were rewarded with positive and accurate coverage in broadcast and print outlets. One story that ran in the *Cincinatti Enquirer* was particularly noteworthy because of the headline: "Community Searches for New Direction: 'Solutions do Exist,' Participants Hear, But Change Won't Be Easy" (Aldridge, 2001). The fact that the story ran with the word solutions in the headline indicated to PolicyLink that its message was getting through and gave further impetus to its communications efforts.

As part of the aftermath of September 11, message development around community-centered policing has taken on a whole new focus. While there is still a need for police reform in localities around the country, the impact of September 11 has changed the landscape, at least for now. Suddenly, in cities such as New York where relationships with police officers and communities of color traditionally have been strained, there is a newfound respect for the police that forces us to reexamine the ways we pitch stories to the local media there. Yet, advocates and reformers recognize that the problems that existed before September 11 continue to exist. PolicyLink communications staff acknowledge that their work in this area will be difficult. Realizing its importance, however, they are committed to continuing to find ways to increase public knowledge about the positive policing models that exist while being sensitive themselves to the facts of the tragedy, in particular, the reality that many police officers lost their lives trying to save others.

Looking to the Future

In the post–September 11 climate, Americans are in need of good news. Surveys indicate that they are more likely to respond to messages of hope and optimism at this time (Elliott, 2001). Resuming their mantle, PolicyLink and other social change organizations may have an enhanced opportunity to lift up stories about policies and strategies that work and that effect policy change. PolicyLink will continue to work with other national and local organizations to build capacity to tell the stories of what works. It will help to develop the expertise of local leaders to serve as media spokespeople. It will continue to educate the media about pressing social issues through the release of informative, thought-provoking publications. PolicyLink is clear about the fact that achieving social justice requires understanding and working with the multifaceted and ever-changing media environment, advancing public knowledge, and building public will to create an inclusive and just society for all Americans is an attainable goal.

Conclusion and Lessons Learned

The experience of PolicyLink has shown that it is possible to get positive and accurate media coverage in an environment that may not be the most accommodating. The challenge is to offer interesting, accurate, thought-provoking information. In a climate where news organizations are obsessed with getting stories first, PolicyLink and other socially conscious organizations must be sure to get stories right. They must think creatively to capture attention and spark interest.

In addition, news organizations, particularly at the local level, are searching for ways to be more relevant and responsive to the needs of their communities. They are willing to put more energy into positive stories and focus on solutions. At the same time, social change organizations have a role to play in making the media more accountable and responsive. They can do this by: raising issues of equity and inclusion; pushing the media to cover racial issues in deeper, more probing ways; lifting up the policy context; changing the frame through which stories are told; and focusing on solutions. Opportunities are there, and only by seizing them will social justice be achieved.

10

THE FUTURE FOR ECONOMICALLY DISTRESSED COMMUNITY–HIGHER EDUCATION PARTNERSHIPS

DAVID N. COX AND MELISSA PEARCE

This chapter will assess trends in community–higher education institution (HEI) partnerships. While such partnerships are appearing globally, the main focus of this assessment will be on future partnerships in the United States. Before discussing the future, it is useful to note that the idea of community-HEI partnerships is not new. Bender and others provide descriptions of community-HEI partnerships from the Middle Ages to the present (Bender, 1988; Cisneros, 1996; Cox, 2000). The purpose of this chapter will be to provide a brief description of the current status of partnerships and offer an assessment of about their future from two perspectives, a view from HEIs and a view from community.

Higher Education Perspective

The past fifteen to twenty years have seen increased interest in community-HEI partnerships in the United States. The changes have been in type and number (Maurrasse, 2001, 2002). A variety of forms of community-HEI partnerships have existed for many years and indeed centuries. Examples include contracts for research and services, public service, joint venture partnerships, co-production of services, and service learning. The type of partnership of focus for this chapter though is on a particular type of partnership, partnerships between higher education institutions and economically distressed neighborhoods aimed at economic and social enhancement for residents of those communities. Properly executed, the partnerships involve shared participation by community residents and higher education faculty members and students in the selection, design, implementation, and evaluation of programming and policies (Feld, 1998; Reardon, 1998).

Growth in the number of these partnerships was in part stimulated by a series of criticisms of the performance of HEIs in the 1980s. Some were aimed at the failures of HEIs in urban areas to be good neighborhoods. HEIs were seen as distant from and in some cases the direct causes of economic distress in the urban settings in which they are located. Other criticisms were aimed at the fundamental roles of HEIs in society. Their contributions are to include the conduct of research leading to new knowledge, the transfer of knowledge to society, and through that research and transfer support for a democratic and socially just society (Benson, Harkavy, and Puckett, 2000; Benson and Harkavy, 2000). Essentially, the criticisms focused on the failures of HEIs in each of these roles. Distancing itself from society in the name of objectivity, research was separated from the fundamental challenges of society. Pursuit of the dollars and prestige of basic research led HEIs to place less emphasis on instruction and on the relationship between research and instruction. According to critics, that distance and separation was significantly reducing HEI's contribution to a democratic and socially just society (Bok, 1982; Boyer, 1990; Lynton, 1995). The partnerships of focus for this chapter have come to be seen by many as a critical means to address all of those criticisms. They are seen to do so through their impact on three types of participants in the partnerships, neighborhood residents, HEIs, and other community stakeholders.

Benefits for neighborhood stakeholders can be found in two forms, access to more resources and participation in processes expanding human and civic capacities. In the first case, HEI's faculty members, staff, and students are repositories of knowledge and expertise useful for community improvement. Participation in the partnerships gives neighborhood stakeholders access to that knowledge and expertise (Feld, 1998). By their scale and buying power, HEIs are important economic engines in many communities (Cisneros, 1996). Participation in partnerships gives neighborhood stakeholders access to some of those dollars (Berens, 1996; Farrish, 1994). HEIs technical expertise can help neighborhood stakeholders gain access grants and other assistance funds. And partnerships with HEIs can give neighborhood residents access to the political capital and prestige associated with many HEI's, capital and prestige that can be critical for access to local and national public and private resources.

Process benefits may be found in the form of programming and in the resulting civic capacity of neighborhoods residents (Innes, 1996; Potapchuk and Polk, 1994; Rosaldo, 1993). Much programming in the past affecting residents of economically distressed neighborhoods has placed residents in a position of dependency (Hackney, 1986; Harkavy and Puckett, 1991, 1992). Persons outside of the neighborhoods decide the programming needed, the design of the programming, and guide the implementation and evaluation of the programming. In the type of partnership of focus in this chapter, neighborhood stakeholders participate in all phases of the programming process, from identifying needs through design to implementation and evaluation (Feld, 1998). One result is programming that more closely fits neighborhood resident needs and assets and has more effective implementation (Kretzmann and McKnight, 1993). Another result is expansion of the social and political knowledge of residents by that participation. The product is expanded civic capacity among neighborhood stakeholders (Putnam, 1993).

HEIs may be community colleges, four-year colleges, and universities. Their foci span the range of undergraduate and graduate, public and private, religious or secularly supported, or teaching and research-focused HEIs. HEI partners may be located within, adjacent to, or at some distance from the partner communities.

Benefits for HEIs can be seen in very practical terms and in terms of their roles in society. Regarding the practical, the performance and survival of HEIs can be affected by the immediate environment in which they are located. Many HEIs are located in urban settings and surrounded by economically distressed communities. As Harkavy and others have pointed out, HEIs are not mobile (Harkavy, 1997). Surrounding deterioration can make it hard to recruit and retain students, faculty, and staff. One reason HEIs enter community-HEI partnerships with adjacent communities aimed at economic and social enhancement is for their own protection (Cisneros, 1996). Other practical benefits can be found in HEI's search for financial, instructional, and political resources. In the first case, partnerships, whether or not with economically distressed communities, can increase HEI's access to funding through preference by public, foundation, and private sector preferences for collaborative efforts. In the second case, partnerships increase HEI's access for internships and placement opportunities for students and instructional, research, and outreach funding. In the third case, community-HEI partnerships can help to build trust and goodwill with other constituencies such as elected officials and business people encouraging their support for funding and other interests of the HEIs.

Regarding HEI's role in society, special roles for HEIs are the creation and dissemination of knowledge in society. In addition they have an important obligation to address the civic requirements and commitments to social justice of democratic society (Benson and Harkavy, 2000). Community-HEI partnerships enhance HEI's performance of these roles by their contributions to better questions, better data and information used to address those questions, better instruction and reflection, and better dissemination of the resulting knowledge.

We have already noted how participation by neighborhood stakeholders in the identification of needs and assets, design of programming, and implementation and evaluation of programming affects that programming. Those very changes represent learning on the part of HEI partners. Framed somewhat differently, Stokes provides a label for a part of that process describing it as "use-inspired basic research." Knowledge creation, according to Stokes, may come about through applied, basic, investigator curiosity, or use-inspired research (Stokes, 1997). Applied research focuses on the practical: What are real-world problems and what works in treating them? Questions are inspired by real-world needs and opportunities. Basic research focuses on the development of theory. Questions are inspired by gaps or contradictions in theory. Investigator curiosity is just that. Questions are guided by and only inform the investigator.

Use-inspired research, however, involves both theory and application. Attention is given to programs or policies based on real-world needs and opportunities. The purpose of programs and policies though is not only to learn whether they worked, but also if so, why? Or, if they did not work, why did they not work? These are the lessons learned from applied research. Lessons become useful when they can be applied at other times or in other places. Answers to questions about whether or how a project or policy worked requires concepts and relationships generalizable across time and space (Rose, 1991, 1993). That requires theory. Use-inspired basic research thus gives rise to the development of theory. Rather than separate types of research and knowledge, use-inspired basic research creates both applied and basic knowledge (Innes, 1995, 1996). Through their impact in directing research attention to real-world questions, community-HEI partnerships provide the basis for practical use-based research. The product is an especially rich contribution to knowledge, practical knowledge for the communities and society, and theoretical knowledge for academic disciplines.

Better information on which to develop answers to the questions comes through additions to the source of persons selecting, collecting, and interpreting data and information. A history of exploitation, unequal access to information, and other challenges make obtaining valid, reliable information about economically distressed communities difficult (Ahlbrandt, Charney, and Cunningham, 1977; Rosaldo, 1993). Persons selecting and interpreting the information have usually been from outside those communities resulting in stereotypes and social distance in what is observed, how it is interpreted, and what is produced ultimately as knowledge. When community-HEI partnerships result in community members (as well as HEI faculty members, students, and staff) joining together and producing and interpreting data, the result is often new information, different interpretations, and better knowledge (Hyland, Cox, and Martin, 1998; Reardon, 1998).

The partnerships produce better instruction and reflection through their effect on content and pedagogy. The production of better knowledge leads to more relevant and accurate instruction.

Better knowledge has produced changes in curricula including formal degree programs, courses, continuing education courses, and workshops and symposia. As important, the effect of the partnerships on how instruction is conducted has produced many benefits for higher education instruction. Working directly with community partners exposes faculty members and students to knowledge, experiences, and the values of persons outside of the formal classroom. That exposure to different life experiences and circumstances, different values, and different expectations broadens students' and faculty members' understanding of community and related issues (Markus, Howard, and King, 1993). Moving outside the classroom produces different relationships between students and faculty members. No longer the sole source of information for students, faculty members must develop new methods to guide discovery and learning. Facing firsthand real-world problems, students are encouraged to discover the interrelationships between issues and solutions that overcome the fragmentation of knowledge produced by HEIs structured around disciplines (Kolb, 1984). Through collaboration with community residents and stakeholders, students and faculty members learn about cooperation and collaboration (Campus Compact, 2000; Kupiec, 1993).

More fundamental, the partnerships affect students' and even faculty members' views of themselves and their relationship to society. Firsthand experiences of engagement contribute to an understanding of the interrelationships and connectedness of all in society. The compartmentalized and disciplinary separation within HEI programs of study can make that interrelatedness difficult to communicate and understand. The experience for many involved in the partnerships has been to produce a lifelong social commitment to address issues of community and especially the issues of distressed communities (Dewar and Isaac, 1998).

Finally, community-HEI partnerships increase the dissemination of new knowledge about the issues they address by reaching new audiences as well as through their access to new media for communication. Information in any setting flows through formal and informal channels. Formal channels for dissemination within a community may include workshops, the distribution of reports, distribution of newsletters, and presentations at community meetings. Informal channels involve the pattern of interpersonal connections and communications within a community. Community-HEI partnerships improve the opportunity for HEIs to disseminate knowledge by improving their access to both channels. As partners, HEIs become regular participants and contributors to formal channels offered through community partners such as newsletters, reports, and workshops. Neighborhood residents active in the partnerships are commonly active participants in informal community networks. Access to those residents through the partnerships provides HEIs an entry point for dissemination through those networks (Brown and Nylander, 1999).

Regarding other stakeholders, many actors may be involved in or impacted by community improvement efforts in an economically distressed community at any given place or time (Mollenkopf, 1983; Swanstrom, 1993). They may include government leaders, nonprofit agencies, developers, and local foundations. As with neighborhood residents and HEIs, many of these actors are seeking additional resources in the form of funding and technical assistant to support community improvement activities. Partnerships help to produce resources by reducing duplication and costs, improving access to funding for comprehensive efforts, and leveraging additional resources. By joining a partnership, members may acquire resources that would otherwise need to be purchased. Students enrolled in courses or seeking practical experience are a source of talented, low-cost labor. Technical assistance costs for other partners may be lowered by in-kind contributions of faculty and student time as a part of HEIs regular instructional, research, and outreach budgets.

Many funders at all levels—federal, state, and local—favor the comprehensive efforts at community improvement that partnerships can provide. Entering a partnership helps actors to gain access to those resources. Funders seeking to support neighborhood improvement can require partners, including HEIs, to contribute resources to compete for and receive their funding. As a result, the partnerships become a means to leverage and thereby increase the reach of their resources.

Based on the realization or expectation of these benefits, there has been a rise in the number and attention to partnerships between communities and HEIs including economically and socially distressed communities over the past two decades. A notable example can be found in interest and participation in the U.S. Department of Housing and Urban Development's Community Outreach Partnership Center (COPC) Program. The COPC Program aims at exactly the type of partnership of interest to this chapter. HEIs partner with residents of economically and socially distressed neighborhoods to address community identified challenges and program opportunities. Despite a demanding application process, the program receives on average 110 to 120 applications per year for about fourteen grants. While about 125 HEIs have received funding since the program's inception in 1995, the number of applicants continues to remain high and grow. Clearly there is substantial interest in HEI partnerships with economically and socially distressed communities.

Other indicators of interest in the partnerships can be found in the appearance and efforts of national organizations in support of the partnerships. Campus Compact was founded in 1985 to further the civic purposes of higher education. To do so, Campus Compact promotes community service aimed at developing students' citizenship skills and values, encourages partnerships between campuses and communities, and assists faculty who seek to integrate public and community engagement into their teaching and research. Many of those partnerships and activities are with the economically and socially distressed communities of focus in this chapter. The rapid growth of the coalition to the 850 college presidents who make up the Campus Compact membership today is evidence of interest in the partnerships. In 1998, the Fannie Mae Foundation directly funded fifteen partnerships between HEIs and economically and socially distressed communities around the country. Under the framework of the Council of Independent Colleges (CIC), the Consortium for the Advancement of Private Higher Education (CAPHE) provided grants to thirteen private colleges in 2001 to establish partnerships with community organizations that can enhance experiential learning activities while addressing community needs. To address disincentives for HEI faculty members to participate in these and other partnerships with communities, the American Association of Higher Education (AAHE) created a Forum on Faculty Roles and Rewards in 1991. Interest in the Forum's activities can be found in the growth of an annual convention on faculty roles and rewards from a few hundred to several thousand within a ten-year span.

Many other associations have either developed special sections to promote community-HEI partnerships or are newly formed for the specific purpose of promoting the partnerships. Long standing national associations such as the American Association of State College and Universities (AASCU), the American Association of Colleges and Universities (AACU), and the National Association of State Universities and Land Grant Colleges (NASULGC) have special commissions and committees exploring means of and making recommendations for encouraging member institutions' participation in partnerships with communities. Community-campus partnerships are the sole focus for the recently formed Association for Community–Higher Education Partnerships (ACHEP) and the Campus-Community Partnerships for Health (CCPH). Promoting partnerships between economically and socially distressed communities and HEIs is the specific purpose of ACHEP. Another recently formed association, the National Consortium for Community-University Partnerships (NCCUP) was created in part through a partnership with a national association of community based agencies, the National Congress on Community Economic Development (NCCED). In sum, the expected and realized benefits from the partnerships would appear to have given rise to a number of efforts to sustain and expand the partnerships.

The Future of Community-HEI Partnerships

If the partnerships are demonstrating benefits to community stakeholders and HEIs and if recognition of those benefits is giving rise to a number of organized efforts working to sustain and expand the partnerships, one could conclude that the future for the partnerships is bright. Indeed, as an advocate for the partnerships, I would hope that will be the case. However, trends in selected indicators from the past are not enough to understand fully the present or project to the future. Other factors may be at work to thwart or alter what might seem to be the current path.

A useful framework for identifying those factors can be found in the social movement theory. Given their import in bringing attention to many of the fundamental issues in civil, gender, and labor rights in the United States, it may seem presumptuous to use our understanding of social movements to assess economically and socially distressed community partnerships with HEIs. Insights from the definition and analysis of social movements and social movement organizations though can provide useful guides for the task. And, as with social movements, the partnerships are associated with efforts by groups to expand democratic practices and achieve social justice (De Leon, 1988).

Turning to social movement theory, Lofland (1996) has defined social movements as: "associations of persons making idealistic and moralistic claims about how human, personal, or group life ought to be organized that, *at the time of their claims-making,* are marginal or excluded from mainstream society—the then dominant constructions of what is realistic, reasonable, and moral." He goes on to add, "The core feature is a *claim about reality* that is, *at the time of its assertion* defined as improper, threatening, or in some other manner not respectable or otherwise meriting serious consideration." Certainly partnerships aiming at the improvement of the lives and opportunities of residents of economically and socially distressed communities can be seen as an idealistic and moralist claim about how human, personal, or group life ought to be organized. The aim of the partnerships is to improve the relevance and quality of knowledge produced and disseminated by HEIs. The means of doing so through real partnerships are aimed at improving the civic performance of HEIs, as well as acknowledging idealistic and moralistic claims. The number of associations just identified who espouse these aims is evidence of a broad effort in support of the partnerships. In these instances, the fit between the partnerships and social movement theory seems straightforward and clear.

Regarding the task of addressing the future, components of the definition of social movements and social movement theory point to questions about current trends and that future for the partnerships. Two issues are especially salient. One, by definition, residents of economically and socially distressed communities are "marginal or excluded from mainstream society." That marginality and exclusion poses at least two challenges to the sustainability and expansion of the partnerships. First, making the changes required to move residents of those communities from marginality to some form of mainstream requires an enormous amount of energy, time, and resources. Though they may have assets in many forms (social, historical, skills, etc.), residents of the neighborhoods have limited resources. Likewise, HEIs have limited resources. Due to demographic patterns the number of students expected to enter HEIs is expected to rise in the coming decade. At the same time, the current slowdown or decline in the economy is reducing revenues for HEIs in the form of tuition payments by students and parents, tax revenues for publicly supported HEIs, and endowment funds for all types of HEIs. The result is increased financial stress for HEIs for some time into the future. Additionally, amidst declining domestic funding and increased competition among national priorities, there are signs of a reduction in the federal government's support for the partnerships. As an example, the COPC Program is currently the only federal program specifically designed to support economically and socially distressed community partnerships with HEIs. However, it has barely survived having been zeroed out of the budget and only reinstated at the last moment in the appropriations process the past three fiscal years. If community-HEI partnerships come to be seen as a cost to HEIs and if external sources of support disappear, it may become difficult to sustain the partnerships or at least sustain them at the level to which they have grown the past few years.

Second and more fundamental, the changes required to address the needs and opportunities of residents of economically and socially distressed communities involve changes in "how human, personal, or group life ought to be organized." That will often mean changes in prevailing public policies as well as the governing structure in any given community. As prestigious and powerful actors in their own right, HEIs are commonly integral parts of the very public policies and governing structures of the communities that may require change. As a subtle but significant indicator of that imbalance in power, a review of the references following this chapter shows that virtually every item written about the partnerships has been written by someone who is a faculty or staff member of a HEI. The voice of community-HEI partnerships is the view from HEIs, not community partners.

As one step in addressing this bias, an additional section of this chapter provides one community resident partner's view of community-HEI partnerships. In general, the community resident is positive and optimistic about the benefits for community through the partnerships. Indeed, at one point she holds community residents responsible for not at times being more active in insisting on HEIs to partner with communities. However, she also strongly expresses a sense of HEI responsibility for community conditions. And, her emphasis on the need for the partnerships to build power for both community residents and HEIs speaks to the concern by community partners about power inequities within the partnerships.

Returning to the central point, HEIs may be or see themselves as beneficiaries of existing policies and structures of power. Given the youth of the economically and socially distressed community-HEI partnerships, it is still not clear whether or how many HEIs will be prepared to spend the political capital required to bring about the changes required to improve the lives and opportunities of residents of economically and socially distressed communities. That is especially the case if those changes are seen in some way to diminish advantages the HEIs believe they receive in the status quo. Where they do not support those efforts, they will defeat the purposes of the partnerships.

The question of willingness to change the status quo leads to the second issue suggested by social movement theory. Harkavy and others have described how U.S. research universities have formed a dominant model of how HEIs are to perform in society (Harkavy, 1997). That focus has especially turned to basic research related to defense in response to post–World War II federal funding. In the language of social movement theory, the dominant construction is that a definition of research and thereby scholarship is limited to those activities that draw their questions from theory and expand that theory for a set of peer researchers. Real-world questions are not appropriate stimuli for research questions. Research is conducted by specially trained disciplinary experts. The only relevant audience and appropriate judge of the quality of that research are peer researchers.

As critics of that model have described, that has come to be seen as the "reality" of research, scholarship, and the role of HEIs in society (Bok, 1982; Boyer, 1990; Lynton, 1995). As further evidence of that "reality," faculty roles and rewards have been structured to encourage that form of inquiry. Tenure and promotion are based on the volume of a researcher's publications in peer (defined as other faculty researchers) reviewed journals and the level of external dollars the researcher generates in support of that research. Likewise, HEI's reputations are based on those two criteria.

A consequence has been to turn research attention away from the social and economic issues of communities and of the civic roles and functions of HEIs as a part of those communities. The role of HEIs in society has been redefined. Theory rather than practical or real-world experiences drive research inquiry. Collaboration and interaction with neighborhoods and community residents is seen as a threat to the "objectivity" required by basic research in directing the research questions to be addressed and the conduct of the research. Engagement by faculty members and students leading to modeling and learning civic behavior on the part of HEI and community participants is given less value and actually discouraged in relation to conducting disengaged basic research. HEIs become increasingly disconnected from real-world conditions and issues of communities. In some cases that disengagement has occurred from the very neighborhoods in which HEI campuses are located (Harkavy and Puckett, 1992).

Faced with these challenges, a current and growing restraint on resources, the potential threat to current structured privileges of HEIs in communities needing change, and the challenges of the partnerships to current definitions of what is defined and valued as research in HEIs, the future growth and development of the partnerships is not assured. There are reasons to argue that recent growth in the partnerships reflects early enthusiasm in an idea that, faced with significant resistance to change, may well recede. Not all social movements succeed (Collins and Hornsby-Smith, 2002; Petchey et al., 1998).

However, social movement theory does point to reasons to be encouraged about the direction of development of the partnerships in the future. For one, social movements spring from different people's perceptions of what is important and problematic in society

(Lofland, 1996). Present growing levels of economic and social distress in communities throughout the United States will continue to lead to pressures and demands on HEIs to address that distress. Given many early successes, those pressures and demands are likely to produce community and political support for the partnerships.

For another, we have noted social movements involve claims about what is "real" and appropriate. In that regard, efforts are continuing to expand the meaning of research appropriate for HEIs beyond basic theory driven inquiry (Adams, 1991; Ansley and Gaventa, 1997; Citrin, 2001; Glassick, Humber, and Maeroff, 1997; Rosaen, Foster-Fishman, and Fear, 2001). They include efforts at articulating the range of elements of scholarship beyond basic research and traditional classroom lecturing (Glassick, Humber, and Maeroff, 1997; Lynton, 1995). They include efforts to reconceptualize our understanding of activities that constitute research beyond theory and laboratory driven inquiry (Schon, 1995; Stokes, 1997). They also include efforts aimed at helping participants in the partnerships implement these changes in communities and HEIs (Driscoll and Lynton, 1999).

In sum, these efforts represent a third aspect related to social movement theory. Ultimately, social movements succeed through collective behavior. The behaviors may take a variety of forms (Gerlach and Hine, 1983). However, the creation and presence of a number of organizations or named associations that see themselves as working toward a common end is to some a defining characteristic of a social movement (Marwell and Oliver, 1984). The development of organized effort is important as a symptom of the level of pressure for change. It can also be critical to sustaining action to bring about change in the face of resistance to the status quo (Gamson, 1990; Lofland, 1996). The large number of organizations advocating for some aspect of the partnerships suggests there is strong support for the partnerships and their goals for economically and socially distressed communities and HEIs. Types of organizations advocating for the partnerships vary from long-standing well-established groups such as AAHE, AASCU, and NASULGC to newer more fragile groups such as ACHEP and CCPH. If they each continue their advocacy they will represent a strong force toward continuing the partnerships. Should they be able to coalesce or collaborate in the effort, in spite of the several challenges, the movement will be more likely to achieve success (Gamson, 1990). The future for partnerships between economically distressed communities and HEIs is indeed promising.

Community Perspective

The trend toward Community Partnerships with Neighborhoods and Higher Education Institutions continues to grow and develop as the participants in the partnerships learn about the mutual benefits the partnerships provide. The appreciation of these mutual benefits allows for a once tenuous relationship to evolve into a working partnership that will make better use of the strengths and resources of each member. This now-working relationship helps forge a collaborative partnership, which promises to yield positive results for all its participants.

The benefits and positive results for the communities are illustrated in a stronger and more respected voice for their neighborhoods. Other benefits include assistance curtailing of crime, redevelopment and revitalization of dilapidated homes, and removal of undesirable businesses. This is not to say that neighborhoods have no power without involvement in a partnership such as this, but that a partnership with a HEI can be the means to utilize the power and strength the neighborhood has more effectively. It is also a means of broadening the power base they have to create other partnerships successfully, both temporary and long lasting, that may be influential in achieving desired changes in the entire community.

Creating partnerships between community-based organizations, HEIs, local governments, school districts, and public housing authorities that work along with neighborhood leaders helps improve the economic, social, and physical conditions of their neighboring communities (Carr, 1999). This becomes a positive for neighborhoods but also for HEIs. It is easier to market a HEI to potential students, staff, and faculty if there is a positive environment in and around their campuses (Cox and Pearce, 2002). Parents want to send their children to a HEI that is an active participant in its community and not one that is disconnected and uninvolved. Communities in which HEIs are more involved are more likely to have a safer and more appealing environment.

Faculty and staff of HEIs as well as other potential stakeholders of the community want to know they can live near their employment and enjoy and participate in the surrounding community. The impact of declining physical and commercial environments in neighborhoods that surround a HEI acts as a catalyst that can suffocate the stability required to generate and maintain the economics needed for successful community building and growth. Decline begins when residents of a community take their purchasing power away from businesses in the neighborhood. This pattern and accompanying attitude leads professionals and high-status workers to leave these communities (Gladwell, 2000). However, keeping incomes in the community creates a demand by the residents of that community for the city to service that community regularly. The demand for service protects the community and forces the city to make sure it provides the required maintenance that it receives tax dollars to provide. The result is streets are in repair, streetlights work, garbage is picked up, and services supplied by the cities are implemented on a regular basis.

HEIs are becoming powerful engines for change. Few institutions have more to contribute, or more at stake, in the revitalization of the neighborhoods around them than HEIs because they cannot simply pack up and relocate. However it was not until urban problems—physical decay and rising crime—began to directly affect HEI's ability to recruit and retain students, faculty, and staff that many HEIs could no longer ignore those problems. Today, many urban universities tie their missions to the areas in which they are situated and provide services to the surrounding communities (Carr, 1999). Combining HEIs with neighborhood and community-based organizations in partnerships can result in a powerful and effective relationship. The changes created by a partnership of this caliber can have a positive and more focused impact on every level of community development.

One area of community development that would benefit from the community and HEI partnership is the education of our youth. Every neighborhood needs excellent schools in which to educate its children and to maintain stability. Stability is a key to positive community development because all the components that make and keep communities strong are intertwined inside the concept of stability.

Families create a stronger economic base to support the businesses in the community, and excellent schools keep families in the neighborhood. It is a cyclical effect that can be a source of strength or weakness in community development. The impact of faculty flight to "safer ground" (with better public schools and services) has a direct impact on the community schools in and around the neighborhoods of the HEI (Harkavy, 1998). Community partnerships with HEIs are marvelous instruments in that they can have a direct positive impact on the cycle that drives positive community growth. The participants in the partnership have a shared interest and concern to watch for stumbling blocks as they surface and to address them immediately; whereas waiting for outside sources may cause unnecessary delays creating more difficult problems that require a higher degree of attention. A benefit to the community from the partnership in the education of its children is the sense of empowerment generated by listening to the neighborhood voice in the management of all aspects of its community, especially the education of the young people.

Community partnerships with HEIs are an opportunity to combine academics with action. "The crisis of the American city," Harkavy writes, "is testimony enough that the self-contained, isolated university will no longer suffice" (Harkavy, 1998a). Engagement with the community for the purpose of building successful partnerships has to be embraced and long-term change has to exist in the curricula of HEIs in order to have the greatest impact because then the results are sustainable, the courses create an ongoing vehicle for future students to keep doing the work.

Communities around HEIs are often changing, sometimes improving, sometimes declining. It would be easy to place full responsibility of decline on HEIs; indeed they are largely responsible for the declines that take place. However, some responsibility also rests with citizens for allowing the negative impacts of HEIs and the decline to occur. It is difficult if a community feels powerless to stop negative growth from taking hold and flourishing, but giving up and abandoning the community instead of standing up to protect it is when the neighborhoods must hold themselves accountable. The commitment of the community partner and the HEI must be to civic engagement and dedication to the protection of the community as well as the rebuilding and revitalization of the individual neighborhoods, communities, and cities. The practice of all participants in the partnership should be the commitment to community—building for the benefit of the community, the HEI, and the city.

In *The Twenty-First Century City* by Goldsmith, Theodore Hershberg is quoted as saying that America's cities are on greased skids. "All of America's cities are on greased skids. What differentiates one from another is the angle of descent. And unless there is a major shift in public policy, America will lose all of its major cities" (Goldsmith, 1999). City leadership along with community partnerships with HEIs can and must change the angle of descent to see successful and positive growth. Community partnerships with HEIs can and must be proactive in preventing the continued negative shift, but they must also work together to change the angle upward and forward. The community-based partnership with neighborhoods and HEIs must continue to work together to build the power base and achieve the maximum result in the sustaining and defining of borders.

One example of expanding the power base through partnerships occurs by combining resources of community residents, HEIs, and other partners such as local investors and financial advisors. Doing so provides added financial and statistical information to aid in decision making. Including community residents in the process along with other organizations such as civic groups, local utilities, faith-based agencies, city services, investors, and politicians is a key element in the process of building neighborhoods.

The work to rebuild and restore the communities (which are the strength and foundation of our country), must take place in steps—block-by-block, community-by-community, town-by- town, city-by-city, county-by-county, and state-by-state. The practice of community building through partnerships can only serve to strengthen this nation and create in every citizen the desire to participate in and be heard by his or her community. The foundations of our cities and communities must be reinforced with community support and strengthened with community spirit. When a city, neighborhood, or state falters it is up to all the citizens and community members to participate in making it strong again. Partnerships that utilize all the power and resources available to them, especially the use of the HEI, will be able to produce stronger neighborhoods and communities.

Changing times are the driving force behind partnerships, collaborations, and alliances between neighborhoods and HEIs. Services once considered the government's business now are being taken on by nonprofit organizations, private vendors, and higher education institutions. Despite the growth in these partnerships, effective implementation and understanding must be improved (Maurrasse 2001). This must be a priority of all members of the partnership. Hard work, dedication, and support by the leadership of the neighborhood and the HEI of its members will allow the partnership to work together to build and sustain strong and healthy communities.

Notes

Introduction

1. David Bolt, and Ray Crawford, *The Digital Divide: Computers and Our Children's Future* (New York: TV Books LLC, 2000). Benjamin M. Compaine, *The Digital Divide: Facing a Crisis or Creating a Myth?* (Cambridge: MIT Press, 2001). Pippa Norris, *The Digital Divide: Civic Engagement, Information Poverty, and the Internet Worldwide.* (Cambridge, UK: Cambridge University Press, 2001). Donald A. Schon, Bish Sanyal, and William J. Mitchell, *High Technology and Low-Income Communities: Prospects for the Positive Use of Advanced Information Technology.* (Cambridge: MIT Press, 1997). William Wersch, *Disconnected: Haves and Have-Nots in the Information Age* (New Brunswick: Rutgers University Press, 1996).
2. Edmund Burke, *Corporate Community Relations: The Principle of Neighbor of Choice* (Westport, CT: Praeger, 1999). James E. Austin, *The Collaboration Challenge: How Nonprofits and Businesses Succeed Through Strategic Alliances* (San Francisco: Jossey-Bass Publishers, 2000).
3. Amy Domini, *Socially Responsible Investing: Making a Difference and Making Money* (Chicago: Dearborn Financial Publishing, 2001).
4. David Maurrasse, *Beyond the Campus: How Colleges and Universities Form Partnerships with Their Communities* (New York: Routledge, 2001). Earnest L. Boyer, *Scholarship Reconsidered: Priorities of the Professoriate* (: Carnegie Foundation for the Advancement of Teaching, 1997).
5. Marc J. Epstein, and Bill Birchard, *Counting What Counts: Turning Corporate Accountability to Competitive Advantage* (Reading: Perseus Books, 2000). Lawrence E. Mitchell, *Corporate Irresponsibility: America's Newest Export* (New Haven: Yale University Press, 2001). Shirley Sagawa, and

Eli Segal, *Common Interest, Common Good: Creating Business and Social Sector Partnerships* (Boston: Harvard Business School Press, 1999).

6. Katherine S. Newman, *No Shame in My Game: The Working Poor in the Inner City* (New York: Vintage Books, 1999).

7. Marc J. Epstein, and Bill Birchard, *Counting What Counts: Turning Corporate Accountability to Competitive Advantage* (Reading: Perseus Books, 2000), Lawrence E. Mitchell, *Corporate Irresponsibility: America's Newest Report* (New Haven: Yale University Press, 2001). Sagawa, and Segal, *Common Interest, Common Good.* R.V.A. Sprout, and J.H. Weaver, "International Distribution of Income: 1960–1987," *Kyklos 45, 2* (1992): 237–85.

8. Epstein, and Birchard, *Counting What Counts.* Mitchell, *Corporate Irresponsibility.* Sagawa, Segal, *Common Interest, Common Good.* Sprout, and Weaver, "International Distribution of Income: 1960–1987."

9. Robert D. Putnam, *Bowling Alone: The Collapse and Revival of American Community* (New York: Touchstone, 2000).

10. Elliott Sclar, and Richard Leone, *You Don't Always Get What You Pay For: The Economics of Privatization* (Ithaca: Cornell University Press, 2000).

11. Sagawa, and Segal, *Common Interest, Common Good.*

12. Maurrasse, *Beyond the Campus.* David Maurrasse, *Listening to Harlem* (New York: Routledge, forthcoming).

13. Arthur Charity, *Doing Public Journalism* (New York: Guilford Press, 1995). D. Hazen, and J. Winokur, *We the Media: A Citizens Guide to Fighting for Media Democracy* (New York: The New Press, 1997). Gene Roberts, Thomas Kunkel, and Charles Layton, *Leaving Readers Behind: The Age of Corporate Newspapering* (Fayetteville: The University of Arkansas Press, 2001).

14. Richard D. Margerum, "Collaborative Planning: Building Consensus and Building a Distinct Model of Practice," *Journal of Planning Education and Research* 21 (2002): 237–53. David E. Booher, and Judith Innes, "Network Power in Collaborative Planning," *Journal of Planning Education and Research* 21 (2002): 221–36.

15. Penda Hair, *Louder than Words: Lawyers, Communities, and the Struggle for Justice* (New York: The Rockefeller Foundation, 2001).

16. Earnest L. Boyer, *Scholarship Reconsidered: Priorities of the Professoriate* (Princeton: Princeton University Press, Carnegie Foundation for the Advancement of Teaching, 1997).

17. S.B. Detmar et al., "Health-Related Quality-of-Life Assessments and Patient-Physician Communication: A Randomized Controlled Trial," *Journal of the American Medical Association* 288, 23 (2002): 3027–34.

18. Phyllis Kansiss. *Making Local News* (Chicago: University of Chicago Press, 1991). J. Rosen, *What Are Journalists For?* (New Haven: Yale University Press, 1999).

19. Mitchell, *Corporate Irresponsibility.*

20. However, in this current economy, a great deal of debate around "foundation payout" has emerged, suggesting that the legal required amount is too low. This discussion has recently entered the House of Represen-

tatives and the *Harvard Business Review*. As Congress discusses a bill, Bill Bradley and partners from McKenzie speculate about how best to leverage existing resources in the nonprofit sector.
21. Chuck Collins, Pam Rogers, and Joan P. Garner, *Robin Hood Was Right: A Guide to Giving Your Money for Social Change* (New York: W. W. Norton & Company, 2000).

Chapter 1

1. Socially responsible business is defined here as the practice by a business of direct responsibilities to employees, shareholders, customers, suppliers, and to the communities where it conducts business and serves markets. Laurie Regelbrugge, "Business and Civil Society: Reflections on Roles, Responsibilities, and Opportunities at the Dawn of a New Century," in *Promoting Corporate Citizenship: Opportunities for Business and Civil Society Engagement*, ed. Laurie Regelbrugge (Washington, D.C.: CIVICUS, 1999), 10. Non-governmental organizations are defined here as non-violent, voluntary citizens' groups that exist outside of the business and governmental sectors.
2. Howard Harris, "Spirituality at Work: Some Australian Observations," *Business and Professional Ethics Journal* 20, no. 1 (2001): 45.
3. Ibid., 46.
4. www.unitedway.org.
5. John Ruggie, (13 October 2000), "Remarks on the Global Compact to the NGO Community United Nations, Geneva." [Online] Accessed 20 October 2001; available from: http://www.unglobalcompact.org/un/gc/unweb.nsf/content/ruggiengo.htm.
6. Kofi Annan, "A Compact for the New Century." [Online] Accessed 5 June 2000; available from: http://www.un.org/partners/business/davos.htm.
7. United Nations, (No date), "The United Nations and Civil Society." [Online] Accessed 15 May 2000; available from: http://www.un.org/partners/civil_society/home.htm.
8. Ibid.
9. Gabriela Flora, (June 14, 2001), "Aventis: Global Compact Violator." [Online] Accessed 30 June 2001; available from: http://www.corpwatch.org.
10. Ibid.
11. United Nations, (June 2001), "First Global Compact Newsletter." [Online] Accessed 2 July 2001; available from: http://www.unglobalcompact.org.
12. United Nations. (No date), "Conflict Diamonds." [Online] Accessed 18 October 2001; Available from: http://www.un.org/peace/africa/Diamond.html.
13. The White House, (May 23, 2001), "Executive Order: Additional Measures with Respect to Prohibiting the Importation of Rough Diamonds

from Sierra Leone." [Online] Accessed 25 May 2001; available from: http://www2.whitehouse.gov/news/releases/2001/05/20010523–11.html.

14. United Nations Foundation, (February 8, 2001), "Angola: UN Asks Oil Companies To Help Bring Peace." [Online] Accessed 8 February 2001; available from: http://www.unfoundation.org.

15. David Murphy and Jem Bendell, *In the Company of Partners: Business, Environmental Groups and Sustainable Development Post-Rio* (Bristol, U.K.: The Policy Press, 1997). Additionally, the definition of NGOs used here is "organizations whose stated purpose is the promotion of . . . social goals rather than the achievement or protection of economic power in the marketplace or political power through the electoral process." Jem Bendell, *Terms of Endearment: Business, NGOs and Sustainable Development* (Sheffield, U.K.: Greenleaf Publishing, 2000).

16. Murphy and Bendell, *In the Company of Partners*.

17. Oxfam UK, (April 19, 2001), "Drug Giants Throw in the Towel." [Online] Accessed 19 April 2001; available from: http://www.oxfam.org.uk.

18. U.N. Security Council, (January 19, 2001), "Security Council Meets on HIV/AIDS and Peacekeeping Operations; Hears from Peacekeeping Under-Secretary-General, UNAIDS." [Online] Accessed 2 October 2001; available from: http://www.un.org/News/Press/docs/2001/sc6992.doc.htm.

19. Oxfam UK, "Drug Giants Throw in the Towel."

20. UNAIDS, (2001), "The Global Fund to Fight HIV/AIDS, TB and Malaria." [Online] Accessed 12 October 2001; available from: http://www.globalfundatm.org/.

21. Shankar Vedantam and DeNeen L. Brown, (October 24, 2001), "U.S. Seeks Price Cut From Cipro Maker; Bayer to Announce Pact 'Shortly'." [Online] Accessed 25 October 2001; available from: http://www.washingtonpost.com/ac2/wp-dyn?pagename=article&node=&contentId=A42255–2001Oct23.

22. International Federation of Chemical, Energy, Mine and General Workers' Unions, (December 20, 2001), "New Voluntary Code Announced in Washington and London." [Online] Accessed 23 December 2000; available from: http://www.icem.org/update/upd2000/upd00–97.html.

23. United Nations Foundation, (October 1, 2001), "Child Slavery: Chocolate Industry Aims To Target Labor Practices." [Online] Accessed 1 October 2001; available from: http://www.unfoundation.org.

24. U.S. Representative Eliot Engel, (October 1, 2001), "Harkin-Engel Protocol Adopted by Chocolate Manufacturers to End Child Slave Labor in the Harvesting of Cocoa." [Online] Accessed 1 October 2001; available from: http://www.house.gov/engel/.

25. Thomas Hemphill, "The White House Apparel Industry Partnership Agreement: Will Self-Regulation Be Successful," *Business and Society Review* 104 (1999): 2.

26. Ibid.

27. Ibid.

28. Medea Benjamin, (1999), "What's Fair about the Fair Labor Association?" [Online] Accessed 24 September 2001; available from: http://www.globalexchange.org/economy/corporations/sweatshops/fla.html.

29. Sierra Club, (September 12, 2001), "Statement of Carl Pope, Sierra Club Executive Director." [Online] Accessed 26 September 2001; available from: www.sierraclub.org/update.asp.

30. Esther Kaplan, (February 13–19, 2002), "Spies in Blue, NY Cops Pushed Legal Limits in WEF Protests." *Village Voice*. [Online] Accessed February 25, 2002; available from: http://www.villagevoice.com/issues/0207/kaplan.php.

31. Clifford Orwin, (September 25, 2001), "Anti-Globalization is So Yesterday." [Online] Accessed 2 October 2001; available from: http://www.nationalpost.com/.

32. Ethan B. Kapstein, "The Corporate Ethics Crusade," *Foreign Affairs* 80, no. 5 (2001): 108.

33. Social Investment Forum, (November 4, 1999), "1999 SRI Trends Report." [Online] Accessed 15 February 2000; available from: http://www.socialinvest.org/Areas/News/1999-trends.htm

34. Ibid.

35. Dow Jones Sustainability World Indexes, (October 2001), "Dow Jones STOXX Index Key Facts." [Online] Accessed 24 October 2001; available from: http://www.sustainability-index.com.

36. World Resources Institute and Aspen Institute, (October 2001), "New survey reveals increasing number of MBA programs recognize relevance of social and environmental stewardship." [Online] Accessed 31 October 2001; available from: http://www.wri.org/wri/press/mba_stewardship.html.

37. The University of Nottingham, (December 4, 2000), "Nottingham University Business School to Establish International Centre for Corporate Social Responsibility." [Online] Accessed 5 December 2000; available from: www.nottingham.ac.uk.

38. Office of the U.S. Trade Representative, (October 24, 2000), "U.S. and Jordan Sign Historic Free Trade Agreement." [Online] Accessed 25 October 2000; available from: http://www.ustr.gov/regions/eu-med/middleeast/US-JordanFTA.shtml.

39. Transparency International, (June 2001), "Corruption Indexes and Surveys." [Online] Accessed 21 September 2001; available from: http://www.transparency.org/documents/index.html#cpi.

40. The report's authors state that "the documents show further that the tobacco companies instigated global strategies to discredit and impede WHO's ability to carry out its mission . . . [they] sought to divert attention from the public health issues, to reduce budgets for the scientific and policy activities carried out by WHO, to pit other UN agencies against WHO, to convince developing countries that WHO's tobacco control programme was carried out . . . at the expense of the developing world, to distort the results of important scientific studies on tobacco, and to discredit WHO as an institution."

41. Global Reporting Initiative, (No date), "Who is participating in the GRI?" [Online] Accessed 5 October 2001; available from: http://www.globalreporting.org/AboutGRI/FAQ.htm.

Chapter 2

1. Bourdieu writes, "Our thought categories *contribute* to the production of the world, but only within the limits of their correspondence with preexisting structures. Symbolic acts of naming achieve their power of creative utterance to the extent, and only to the extent, that they propose principles of vision and division objectively adapted to the preexisting divisions of which they are the products. By consecrating what is uttered, such utterance carries its object to that fully attained higher existence which characterizes constituted institutions. In other words, the specific symbolic effect of the representations, which are produced according to schemas adapted to the structures of the world which produce them, is to confirm the established order. A 'correct' representation ratifies and sanctifies the doxic view of the divisions of the social world by representing this view with the perceived objectivity and orthodoxy. Such an act is a veritable act of creation which, by proclaiming orthodoxy in the name of and to everyone, confers upon it the practical universality of that which is *official*." Pierre Bourdieu, "The Force of Law: Toward a Sociology of the Juridical Field," *Hastings Law Journal* 38 (1987): 805, 839.

2. The distinction between "public" and "private" spheres has several different meanings. For example, many feminist writings discuss the division of labor along normative lines of gender and sex and have used the public/private distinction to elucidate the difference between the world of work and government and the realm of social life, domestic work, and family. In more general terms, the public/private divide is often used to distinguish between issues involving the state and its regulation of society and those that are "personal." In this chapter, the term refers to a perceived differentiation between the realms of individual interests and public accountability, recognizing a line between social and economic activities that are performed in furtherance of "the self" and those that foster community growth.

3. Without a doubt, many professionals provide services that help society operate in a cohesive and efficient manner. However, the distinguishing inquiry is not simply if society benefits from these services, but understanding the motivations of one's professional duties and obligations.

4. Karl E. Klare, "The Public/Private Distinction in Labor Law," *University of Pennsylvania Law Review* 130 (1982): 1358.

5. Pierre Bourdieu and Loic J.D. Wacquant, *Invitation to a Reflexive Sociology* (Chicago: University of Chicago Press, 1992), 97.

6. Ibid., 97–98.

7. Priscilla Parhurst Ferguson, "A Cultural Field in the Making: Gastonomy in 19th Century France," *American Journal of Sociology* 104, no. 3 (November 1998): 598.

8. Bourdieu and Wacquant, *Invitation to Reflexive Sociology*, 105.

9. Bourdieu states, "We can indeed, with caution, compare a field to a game (jeu) although, unlike the latter, a field is not the product of a deliberate act of creation, and it follows rules or, better, regularities, that are not ex-

plicit and codified. Thus, we have stakes (enjeux) which are for the most part the product of the competition between players. We have an investment in the game: players are taken in by the game, they oppose one another, sometimes with ferocity, only to the extent that they concur in their beliefs (doxa) in the game and its stakes; they grant these a recognition that escapes questioning. Players agree, by the mere fact of playing, and not by way of a "contract," that the game is worth playing, that it is "worth the candle," and this collusion is the very basis of competition. We also have trump cards, that is, master cards whose force varies depending on the game: just as the relative value of cards changes with each game, the hierarchy of the different species of capital (economic, social, cultural, symbolic) varies across the various fields. In other words, there are cards that are valid, efficacious in all fields—these are the fundamental species of capital—but their relative value as trump cards is determined by each field and even by successive states of the same field." *Ibid.*, 98.

10. See generally www.abanet.org/home.html.
11. Perhaps the quintessential example of privacy in this context is lawyer/client privilege, whereby a lawyer is bound ethically not to divulge publicly any communications that occur between him and the client. For more on this, see Rule 1.6 of the Model Rules and DR 4–101 of the Code.
12. There is little doubt that the stakes are generally much higher in a criminal proceeding, which may justify a need for legal representation exclusive of social needs. For example, in a capital case, the possibility of the death sentence legitimately may lead a lawyer to represent his client without regard to the community because his client's life is on the line. However, in such situations, the public's interest is represented adequately. Since the state is a party to the case (and, in fact, prosecutes the individual), it is endowed by the community to act in its interests.
13. Pierre Bourdieu, *Outline of a Theory of Practice,* (New York: Cambridge University Press, 1977), p. 78.
14. Ibid., 82.
15. Morton J. Horwitz, "The History of the Public/Private Distinction," *University of Pennsylvania Law Review* 130 (1982): 1423, 1425.
16. Ibid., 1426.
17. Klare "Public/Private Distinction," 1417.
18. For more information on Columbia's *pro bono* requirement, see http://www.law.columbia.edu/publicinterest/probono.htm.
19. For more information on the Kirkland and Ellis Fellowship, see http://www.kirkland.com/careers/lawstudents/fellowship.asp?schoolid=35.
20. For more information on the Skadden Foundation, see http://www.skadden.com/siteindex.htm.
21. David J. Maurrasse, *Beyond the Campus: How Colleges and Universities Form Partnerships with their Communities* (New York: Routledge Press, 2001), 181.
22. For more information on CISR, see http://www.maximixingbonds.org.

Chapter 3

The author wishes to thank Carla Tabossi for providing significant assistance in researching and writing this chapter. Sincere thanks are also given to Daniel Esty and Peter Cornelius for providing invaluable editorial feedback.

1. While there are many views on the meaning of environmental sustainability, the concept generally refers to not reducing the ability of the environment to meet the needs of future generations. The broader term, sustainability, addresses environmental and social issues, such as meeting basic human needs and respecting cultural diversity. The two terms are related, not only because they both refer to environmental issues, but also because environmental sustainability probably cannot be achieved without addressing social issues. For example, if basic human needs are not met, people might clear forests (needed for environmental sustainability) to survive in the short term.

2. Following are some of the studies in which positive correlations between environmental and financial performance were found: Konar and Cohen, 2001; Dowell, Hart, and Yeung, 2000; Johnson, Magnan, and Stinson, 1998; Russo and Fouts, 1997; Feldman, Soyka, and Ameer, 1997; Clough, 1997; European Federation of Financial Analysts, 1996; Cohen, Fenn, and Naimon, 1995; White, 1995; Hart and Ahuja, 1994: and Snyder et al., 1993.

3. Greenwashing generally refers to efforts by companies to portray themselves as being environmentally responsible, for the purpose of improving stakeholder relations, without significantly improving actual performance. An example of greenwashing might be when an electric utility focuses its corporate environmental report on building wildlife sanctuaries near its headquarters, but hardly addresses its power plants emissions. The sanctuaries are important, but probably not financially relevant to the firm, as emissions most likely would be.

4. Negative screening involves avoiding investments in certain industry sectors with high environmental risks, such as nuclear power, as well as avoiding investments in sectors such as alcohol and tobacco that investors oppose for ethical reasons. This approach can reduce diversity and increase portfolio risk.

5. For example, a letter from the U.S. Department of Labor to William M. Tartikoff, Senior Vice President and General Counsel of Calvert Group Ltd., dated May 28, 1998, stated that the Department of Labor "has expressed the view that the fiduciary standards of [ERISA] sections 403 and 404 do not preclude consideration of collateral benefits, such as those offered by a 'socially-responsible' fund, in a fiduciary's evaluation of a particular investment opportunity," provided that the investment is equal to or superior to alternative available investments on an economic basis.

6. Information from these databases can be downloaded from the nonprofit Right-To-Know network (www.RTK.net), which has been given authority by the U.S. government to disseminate these data to the general public.

7. More information about EcoValue'21™ and Innovest in general is available at www.innovestgroup.com.

Chapter 4

The work described in this chapter has been supported by two grants from the W. K. Kellogg Foundation—Community DentCare grant and the Northern Manhattan Community Voices Collaborative grant. The authors express appreciation to the Foundation for their support.

1. J. Califano, *Radical Surgery: What's Next for American's Health Care* (New York: Times Books, Random House, Inc., 1994).
2. U.S. Department of Health and Human Services, *Health People 2010* (Conference Edition in Two Volumes) (Washington, D.C., January 2002).
3. Northern Manhattan Community Voices Collaborative, *Mental Health: The Neglected Epidemic, a Report of the Difficult to Cover Services Workgroup* (New York: Columbia University, Center for Community Health Partnerships, May 2001).
4. W. K. Kellogg Foundation, *More than a Market: Making Sense of Health Care Systems. Lessons from Community Voices: Health Care for the Underserved* (Battle Creek, Mich.: W. K. Kellogg Foundation, 2002).

Chapter 5

1. As an aside, research shows that people who have never been in the work force often enter through the retail sector, get good skills, and attach rapidly to the work force. Retail jobs can, in fact, be good opportunities for career advancement.

Chapter 6

1. From 1991 to 1999, Aida Rodriguez was a senior program officer and Deputy Director (1997–1999) of the Rockefeller Foundation's Equal Opportunity Division. The major division foci included: macroeconomic research, job access/job creation research demonstrations, community building and advocacy programs, school reform and advancing the basic rights of minorities in the Unites States.
2. The PRLDEF study is one of three complementary studies of Latino nonprofits in the United States conducted under the sponsorship of Hispanics in Philanthropy. The other two studies were completed by the NEDLC and the Tomas Rivera Center. In this chapter, we present some preliminary evidence from the East Coast that suggests a role intermediaries can play in capacity building. The PRLDEF study focused on the East Coast and surveyed nonprofit organizations in the metropolitan areas of Boston (MA), Miami (FL), Newark (NJ), New York City, Philadelphia (PA), and the state of Connecticut. The goal of the study was

to provide baseline data for the development of strategies to strengthen the Latino nonprofit sector. Data was collected from a total of 336 Latino nonprofit organizations (35% response rate) through the completion of a mail survey. In total, the three studies provide information on over one thousand Latino nonprofits in the United States. A report summarizing the findings from the three surveys will be released by Hispanics In Philanthropy at the end of this year.

3. The National Community Development Initiative (NCDI) is a ten-year effort involving eighteen public and private funders to accelerate the growth, scale, and impact of community development corporations and their activities in twenty-three cities around the country. NCDI funders have two major goals: (1) to assist the development and maturation of local systems that support community development—system change; and (2) to increase the availability of usable long-term financing for CDC-developed projects (Walker and Weinheimer, 1998).

Chapter 7

1. The term "payout" includes qualifying distributions—grants, administrative expenses such as rent and salaries, program related investments, amounts set aside for future charitable projects, and trustee fees. The term "grants payout" includes only grants and excludes all other qualifying distributions. The analysis that follows is mainly concerned with the ratio of grants to assets, which is the significant figure from an economic point of view. This economic payout ratio concept should not be confused with the legal payout ratio concept, which involves total qualifying distributions divided by average assets over the previous five-year period.

2. Nelson compares grants to gross national product, rather than gross domestic product.

3. Following Nelson, "internal growth" from investment return in excess of payout is calculated by first stripping out from 1996 assets all the new gifts over the entire period ($50.98 billion), leaving $40.77 billion as an estimate of what 1996 assets would have been without any new gifts at all. (This is probably an overestimate, since the new gifts also compounded during the period.) The no-gift 1996 asset estimate is then compared with the initial 1977 assets ($31.4 billion) to calculate the rate of compound growth, which is 1.38% annually. (This is probably also an overestimate.) "External growth" is then calculated as the additional asset growth from new gifts that is required to add up to the actual total compound growth of 5.81%, so 1.0138x1.0436=1.0581. Because this calculation tends to overestimate the contribution of internal investment return, it also tends to underestimate the contribution of new gifts. It should be noted that, although the calculation methodology is identical to Nelson's, the data to which it is applied here is somewhat different. Nelson studied the growth of a fixed panel of foundations, while the present analysis is concerned with the growth of the foundation sector as a whole.

4. To ensure comparability, investment returns were taken from DeMarche Associates (1995, Tables 3–5), which explains why the most recent year is 1994. In order to retain a twenty-year time span, the start date was pushed back to 1975. Because of the different time spans, Tables 2 and 3 are not strictly comparable.

5. Figures for total charitable payout are provided for the sake of comparability with DeMarche Associates, Table E-1. From an economic point of view, however, it is not legitimate to add payouts in different years without discounting later years by the time value of money.

Chapter 8

1. The used computers were refurbished and donated to computer centers that provided free computer access to people from low-income communities.

Bibliography

Chapter 1

Annan, K. "A Compact for the New Century." [Online] Accessed 5 June 2000; available from: http://www.un.org/partners/business/davos.htm.

Bendell, J. *Terms of Endearment: Business, NGOs and Sustainable Development.* Sheffield, U.K.: Greenleaf Publishing, 2000.

Benjamin, M. (1999) "What's Fair about the Fair Labor Association?" [Online] Accessed 24 September 2001; available from: http://www.globalexchange.org/economy/corporations/sweatshops/fla.html.

Dow Jones Sustainability World Indexes. (October 2001). "Dow Jones STOXX Index Key Facts." [Online] Accessed 24 October 2001; available from: http://www.sustainability-index.com.

Flora, G. (June 14, 2001). "Aventis: Global Compact Violator." [Online] Accessed 30 June 2001; available from: http://www.corpwatch.org.

Global Reporting Initiative. (No date). "Who is participating in the GRI?" [Online] Accessed 5 October 2001; available from: http://www.globalreporting.org/AboutGRI/FAQ.htm.

Harris, H. "Spirituality at Work: Some Australian Observations." *Business and Professional Ethics Journal* 20, no. 1 (2001): 45.

Hemphill, T. "The White House Apparel Industry Partnership Agreement: Will Self-Regulation Be Successful?" *Business and Society Review* 104 (1999): 2.

International Federation of Chemical, Energy, Mine and General Workers' Unions. (December 20, 2001). "New Voluntary Code Announced in Washington and London." [Online] Accessed 23 December 2000; available from: http://www.icem.org/update/upd2000/upd00–97.html.

Kapstein, E. B. "The Corporate Ethics Crusade." *Foreign Affairs* 80, no. 5 (2001): 108.

Murphy, D. and J. Bendell. *In the Company of Partners: Business, Environmental Groups and Sustainable Development Post-Rio.* Bristol, U.K.: The Policy Press, 1997.

Office of the U.S. Trade Representative. (October 24, 2000). "U.S. and Jordan Sign Historic Free Trade Agreement." [Online] Accessed 25 October 2000; available from: http://www.ustr.gov/regions/eu-med/middleeast/US-JordanFTA.shtml.

Orwin C. (September 25, 2001). "Anti-Globalization is So Yesterday." [Online] Accessed 2 October 2001; available from: http://www.national-post.com/.

Oxfam UK. (April 19, 2001). "Drug Giants Throw in the Towel." [Online] Accessed 19 April 2001; available from: http://www.oxfam.org.uk.

Regelbrugge, L. "Business and Civil Society: Reflections on Roles, Responsibilities, and Opportunities at the Dawn of a New Century." In *Promoting Corporate Citizenship: Opportunities for Business and Civil Society Engagement*, edited by L. Regelbrugge, 10. Washington, D.C.: CIVICUS, 1999.

Ruggie, J. (13 October 2000). "Remarks on the Global Compact to the NGO Community United Nations, Geneva." [Online] Accessed 20 October 2001; available from: http://www.unglobalcompact.org/un/gc/unweb.nsf/content/ruggiengo.htm.

Sierra Club. (September 12, 2001). "Statement of Carl Pope, Sierra Club Executive Director." [Online] Accessed 26 September 2001; available from: www.sierraclub.org/update.asp.

Social Investment Forum. (November 4, 1999). "1999 SRI Trends Report." [Online] Accessed 15 February 2000; available from: http://www.social-invest.org/Areas/News/1999-trends.htm

Transparency International. (June 2001). "Corruption Indexes and Surveys." [Online] Accessed 21 September 2001; available from: http://www.transparency.org/documents/index.html#cpi.

UNAIDS. (2001). "The Global Fund to Fight HIV/AIDS, TB and Malaria." [Online] Accessed 12 October 2001; available from: http://www.globalfundatm.org/.

United Nations. (No date). "Conflict Diamonds." [Online] Accessed 18 October 2001; available from: http://www.un.org/peace/africa/Diamond.html.

United Nations. (June 2001). "First Global Compact Newsletter." [Online] Accessed 2 July 2001; available from: http://www.unglobalcompact.org.

United Nations. (No date). "The United Nations and Civil Society." [Online] Accessed 15 May 2000; available from: http://www.un.org/partners/civil_society/home.htm.

United Nations Foundation. (February 8, 2001). "Angola: UN Asks Oil Companies To Help Bring Peace." [Online] Accessed 8 February 2001; available from: http://www.unfoundation.org.

United Nations Foundation. (October 1, 2001). "Child Slavery: Chocolate Industry Aims To Target Labor Practices." [Online] Accessed 1 October 2001; available from: http://www.unfoundation.org.

The University of Nottingham. (December 4, 2000). "Nottingham University Business School to Establish International Centre for Corporate Social

Responsibility." [Online] Accessed 5 December 2000; available from: www.nottingham.ac.uk.

Vedantam, S. and D. L. Brown, (October 24, 2001). "U.S. Seeks Price Cut From Cipro Maker; Bayer to Announce Pact 'Shortly'." [Online] Accessed 25 October 2001; available from: http://www.washingtonpost.com/ac2/wp-dyn?pagename=article&node=&contentId=A42255–2001Oct23.

The White House. (May 23, 2001). "Executive Order: Additional Measures with Respect to Prohibiting the Importation of Rough Diamonds from Sierra Leone." [Online] Accessed 25 May 2001; available from: http://www2.whitehouse.gov/news/releases/2001/05/20010523–11.html.

World Resources Institute and Aspen Institute. (October 2001). "New survey reveals increasing number of MBA programs recognize relevance of social and environmental stewardship." [Online] Accessed 31 October 2001; available from: http://www.wri.org/wri/press/mba_stewardship.html.

Chapter 3

Blank, Herb D., and C. Michael Carty. "The Eco-Efficiency Anomaly." QED International Associates, Inc., April 30, 2001.

Butz, and Plattner. *Sustainable Investments: An Analysis of Returns in Relation to Environmental and Social Criteria.* Bank Sarasin, 1999.

Center for the Study of Financial Innovation. *Measuring Environmental Risk.* 1994.

Clough, Richard. *Impact of an Environmental Screen on Portfolio Performance: A Comparative Analysis of S&P Stock Returns.* Durham, N.C.: Duke University Press, 1997.

Cogan, Douglas. *Tobacco Divestment and Fiduciary Responsibility, A Legal and Financial Analysis.* Investor Responsibility Research Center, January 2000.

Cohen, M. A., S. A. Fenn, and J. S. Naimon. *Environmental and Financial Performance: Are They Related?* Nashville: Vanderbilt University, Owen Graduate School of Management, 1995.

Cram, Don, and Dinah Koehler. *The Financial Impact of Corporate Environmental Performance: Evidence of the Link between Environmental and Financial Performance.* Working draft, May 2001.

Dowell, Glen, Stuart Hart, and Bernard Yeung, "Do Corporate Global Environmental Standards Create or Destroy Market Value?" *Management Science* 46 (2000).

European Federation of Financial Analysts. "Eco-Efficiency and Financial Analysis: The Financial Analysts View." 1996.

Feldman, S. J., P. A. Soyka, and P. Ameer. "Does Improving a Firm's Environmental Management System and Environmental Performance Result in a Higher Stock Price?" *Journal of Investing* 6 (1997).

Gibson, Virginia L., Bonnie K. Levitt, and Karine H. Cargo). *Overview of Social Investments and Fiduciary Responsibility of County Employee Retirement System Board Members in California.* Chicago, Baker & McKenzie, 2000.

Hart, Stuart L., and Gautam Ahuja. *An Empirical Examination of the Relationship Between Pollution Prevention and Firm Performance.* Ann Arbor: University of Michigan, School of Business Administration, 1994.

ICF Kaiser. *Does Improving a Firm's Environmental Management System and Environmental Performance Result in a Higher Stock Price?* 1996.

Johnson, M. F., M. Magnan, and C. H. Stinson. "Nonfinancial Measures of Environmental Performance as Proxies for Environmental Risks and Uncertainties." 1998.

Konar, S., and M. A. Cohen, "Does the Market Value Environmental Performance?" *Review of Economics and Statistics* 83 (2001).

Koppes, Richard H., and Maureen L. Reilly, "An Ounce of Prevention: Meeting the Fiduciary Duty to Monitor an Index Fund through Relationship Investing." *The Journal of Corporation Law* (spring 1995).

McKeown, William B. "On Being True to Your Mission: Social Investments for Foundations." *Journal of Investing* (winter 1997).

Pava, and Krausz. *Corporate Responsibility and Financial Performance.* 1995.

Repetto, Robert, and Duncan Austin. "Coming Clean: Corporate Disclosure of Financially Significant Environmental Risks." World Resources Institute, 2000.

Russo, M. V., and P. A. Fouts. "A Resource-Based Perspective on Corporate Environmental Performance and Profitability." *Academy of Management Journal* 40 (1997).

Snyder, Jonathan, C.F.A. et al. "The Performance Impact of an Environmental Screen," Winslow Management Company/Eaton Vance, 1993.

Social Investment Forum. "1999 Report on Socially Responsible Investing Trends in the United States." 1999.

Social Investment Forum. "7 Out of 8 Largest Social Funds Get Top Performance Marks for 2000." January 2001.

Solomon, Lewis D., and Karen Coe. "The Legal Aspects of Social Investing by Non-Profits." *Journal of Investing* (winter 1997).

3M. "3M Pollution Prevention Pays: Moving Toward Environmental Sustainability," 1998.

U.S. Environmental Protection Agency. "Environmentally Screened Index Investing." November 1996.

———. "Green Dividends? The Relationship Between Firms' Environmental Performance and Financial Performance." 2000.

White, Mark A. *Corporate Environmental Performance and Shareholder Value.* Charlottesville: University of Virginia, McIntire School of Commerce, November 1995.

World Business Council for Sustainable Development. "Environmental Performance and Shareholder Value." 1997.

Chapter 6

Billitteri, Thomas J. "Technology and Accountability Will Shape the Future of Philanthropy." *The Chronicle of Philanthropy* 12, no. 6 (2000): 10, 16, 20.

Bonilla, Frank, Edwin Melendez, Rebecca Morales, and Maria de los Angeles Torres. *Borderless Borders: U.S. Latinos, Latin Americans, and the Paradox of Interdependence.* Philadelphia: Temple University Press, 1998.

Boris, Elizabeth T. "The Nonprofit Sector in the 1990s." In *Philanthropy and the Nonprofit Sector in a Changing America,* edited by Charles T. Clotfelter and Thomas Ehrlich. Bloomington: Indiana University Press, 1999.

Campoamor, Diana, and William A. Diaz. "Hispanics in Philanthropy and the Nonprofit Sector; An Overview." In *Nuevos Senderos: Reflections on Hispanics and Philanthropy,* edited by Diana Campoamor, William A. Diaz, and Henry A.J. Ramos. Houston: Arte Publico Press, 1999.

Cordero-Guzman, Hector, and Jose G. Navarro. "What do Immigrant Service Providers Say About the Impacts of Recent Changes in Immigration and Welfare Laws." *Migration World* 28, no. 4 (2000): 20–27.

Corporation for Supportive Housing. "Work in Progress: An Interim Report from the *Next Steps: Jobs Initiative.*" May 1997.

Hispanic Federation. Internal Document. Proposal for the Support of the Hispanic Federation's Hispanic Leadership Institute (available upon request). October 2000.

Hodgkinson, Virginia Ann, Murray S. Weitzman, with John A. Abrahams, Eric A. Crutchfield, and David R. Stevenson. *Nonprofit Almanac: Dimensions of the Nonprofit Sector, 1996–1997.* San Francisco: Jossey-Bass Publishers, 1996.

Letts, Christine, William Ryan, and Allen Grossman. *High Performance Nonprofit Organizations: Managing Upstream for Greater Impact.* New York: Wiley, 1999.

Pereira, Joseph A., and Michelle Ronda. "The Latino Nonprofit Sector in the United States and Miami, Florida." Puerto Rican Legal Defense and Education Fund Report. September 2000. Final Report submitted to The Funders Collaborative for Strong Latino Communities and Hispanics in Philanthropy.

Salamon, Lester M., Helmut K. Anheier, Regina List, Stefan Toepler, S. Wojciech Sokolowski and Associates. *Global Civil Society: Dimensions of the Nonprofit Sector.* Baltimore: Johns Hopkins University Press, 1999.

Walker, Christopher, and Mark Weinheimer. *Community Development in the 1990s.* Washington, D.C.: The Urban Institute, 1998.

Wish, Naomi, and Roseanne M. Mirabella. "Curricular Variations in Nonprofit Management Graduate Programs." *Nonprofit Management and Leadership* 9, no. 1 (1998): 99–109.

U.S. Bureau of the Census (1997). *Facts for Hispanic Heritage Month* (Memorandum CB97–FS, 10, September 11).

Web Sites

Corporation for Supportive Housing: www.csh.org
The Enterprise Foundation: www.enterprisefoundation.org
The Hispanic Federation: www.hispanicfederation.org
Local Initiatives Support Corporation: www.liscnet.org
Seedco and the Non-Profit Assistance Corporation: www.seedco.org

Chapter 7

Arnsberger, Paul. "Private Foundations and Charitable Trusts, 1995." *Statistics of Income Bulletin* (winter 1998/1999): 60–104.

Council on Foundations. *Foundation Management Series, Volume 1.* Washington, DC: Council on Foundations, 1998.

Craig, John E., Jr. "In Favor of Five Percent." *Foundation News and Commentary* 40, no. 3 (May/June 1999): 23, 25.

DeMarche Associates, Inc. *Spending Policies and Investment Planning for Foundations: A Structure for Determining a Foundation's Asset Mix.* Washington DC: Council on Foundations, 1995.

Foundation Center. *Foundation Giving: Yearbook of Facts and Figures on Private, Corporate and Community Foundations.* New York: The Foundation Center, 1991–1999 Editions.

Frumkin, Peter. "The Long Recoil from Regulation: Private Philanthropic Foundations and the Tax Reform Act of 1969." *American Review of Public Administration* 28, no. 3 (1998): 226–86.

Nelson, Ralph L. "An Economic History of Large Foundations" In *America's Wealthy and the Future of Foundations,* edited by Teresa Odendahl, 127–77. New York: The Foundation Center, 1987.

Odendahl, Teresa, and Diane Feeney. "Who's Afraid of Increasing Payout?" *Foundation News and Commentary* 40, no. 3 (May/June 1999): 22, 24.

Salamon, Lester M. *Investment and Payout Performance Update.* New York: The Foundation Center, 1991.

Salamon, Lester, and Kenneth Voytek. *Managing Foundation Assets: An Analysis of Foundation Investment Procedures and Performance.* New York: The Foundation Center, 1989.

Schervish, Paul G., and John J. Havens. *New Estimates of the Forthcoming Wealth Transfer.* Chestnut Hill: Boston College Social Welfare Research Institute, 1999.

Chapter 8

BBC News On-Line. "Information Rich Information Poor, Bridging the Digital Divide." 1999.

Bowman, J. "Digital Divide Reality, Fact or Fiction: How Do We Meet the Challenge." *Experts on the Digital Divide* 1, no. 2 (2001).

Bowman, J. "CyberHood Connections: Educational Webmasters and Designing Hypermedia Environments." *Journal of Educational Technology Systems.* Amityville: Baywood Publishing Co., 1996.

Cochran, J. "The Digital Divide Narrows, Technically and Psychologically Solving the Internet Gap Challenge." ABC News, 1999.

Culver, C. "Private Digital Divide Efforts Fall Short." *Interactive Week,* 2000.

Fix, J. L. "Some Are Trapped in a Non-Tech World." Free Press Washington Staff, *Detroit Free Press,* 2000.

Lawrence, J. "DNC Tackles Own Digital Divide," *USA Today* 2002.

National Telecommunication and Information Administration. *Falling Through the Net*. Full Report. 1995. (http://www.ntia.doc.gov/ntiahome/falling thru.html)

National Telecommunication and Information Administration. *Falling Through the Net II: New Data on the Digital Divide*. Full Report. 1997. (http://www.ntia.doc.gov/ntiahome/net2/falling.html)

National Telecommunication and Information Administration. *Falling Through the Net III: Defining the Digital Divide*. Full Report. 1999. (http://www.ntia.doc.gov/ntiahome/digitaldivide/)

Associated Press. "The Booming Net Population." The Center for the Study of Technology and Society, 2001.

The Emerging Digital Economy II, Vice President Gore's Publication.

Schement, J. R. "Democracy Digitized. Federal Communications Commission's new Chairman Michael Powell." *Broadcasting & Cable Magazine*, 2001.

Chapter 9

Aldridge, Kevin. "Community Searches for New Direction." *Cincinatti Enquirer*, 27 June 2001.

Benesch, Susan. "The Rise of Solutions Journalism." *Columbia Journalism Review* (March/April 1998).

Blackwell, Angela Glover. "Holding Onto Harlem." *New York Times*, 12 April 2001.

Dorfman, Lori, and Vincent Schiraldi. *Off Balance: Youth, Race & Crime in the News*. Report from Building Blocks for Youth (www.buildingblocksforyouth.org). 2001.

Elliott, Stuart. "Consumers May Change Behavior as a Result of Terrorist Attacks." *New York Times*, 27 September 2001.

Hewitt, Don. *Tell Me A Story: Fifty Years and 60 Minutes in Television*. New York: Public Affairs, 2001.

Newkirk, Pamela T. "Guess Who's Leaving the Newsrooms." *Columbia Journalism Review* (September/October 2000).

The Pew Center for Civic Journalism. "Survey Pinpoints a Sea Change in Attitudes and Practices." *Civic Catalyst* (summer 2001).

The Pew Center for Civic Journalism. "Civic Journalism: Point-Counterpoint." *Civic Catalyst* (winter 2000).

The Pew Research Center for the People & the Press. *Striking The Balance*. 1999.

PolicyLink. *Community Based Initiatives Promoting Regional Equity*. Oakland: PolicyLink, 2000.

PolicyLink. *Opportunities for Smarter Growth: Social Equity and the Smart Growth Movement*. Oakland: PolicyLink and Miami, FL: Funders Network for Smart Growth and Livable Communities (joint copyright), 1999.

Sengupta, Somini. "Sept. 11 Attack Narrows the Racial Divide." *The New York Times*, 10 October 2001.

Sorkin, Andrew Ross. "NBC Is Paying $1.98 Billion for Telemundo." *New York Times*, 12 October 2001.

Chapter 10

Adams, Carolyn. "Urban Regions as Educational Laboratories." *Metropolitan Universities* (fall 1991): 37–46.

Ahlbrandt, R., M. Charney, and J. Cunningham. "Citizen Perceptions of Their Neighborhoods." *Journal of Housing* 7 (1977): 338–41.

Ansley, F., and J. Gaventa. "Researching for Democracy and Democratizing Research." *Change* 29 (1997): 46–53.

Bender, Thomas, ed. "Introduction." In *The University and the City: From Medieval Origins to the Present*. New York: Oxford University Press, 1988.

Benson, Lee, and Ira Harkavy. "Higher Education's Third Revolution: The Emergence of the Democratic Cosmopolitan Civic University." *Cityscape: A Journal of Policy Development and Research* 5, no. 1 (2000): 47–57.

Benson, Lee, Ira Harkavy, and John Puckett. "An Implementation Revolution as a Strategy for Fulfilling the Democratic Promise of University-Community Partnerships: Penn-West Philadelphia as an Experiment in Progress." *Nonprofit and Voluntary Sector Quarterly* 29, no. 1 (2000): 24–45.

Berens, Gayle. "Campus Partners, Columbus." *Urban Land* 55, no. 4 (1996): 57–60.

Bok, Derek. *Beyond the Ivory Tower: Social Responsibilities of the Modern University*. Cambridge, MA: Harvard University Press, 1982.

Boyer, Ernest L. *Scholarship Reconsidered: Priorities of the Professoriate*. Princeton, NJ: Carnegie Foundation for the Advancement of Teaching, 1990.

Brown, Ralph B., and Albert B. Nylander III. "Community Leadership Structure: Differences Between Rural Community Leaders' and Residents' Informational Networks." *Journal of the Community Development Society* 29, no. 1 (1999): 71–89.

Campus Compact. *Benchmarks for Campus/Community Partnerships*. Providence, RI: Campus Compact, 2000

Carr, James H. "It's Not Just Academic: University-Community Partnerships Are Rebuilding Neighborhoods." *Fannie Mae Foundation Housing Facts & Findings* 1, no. 1 (1999).

Cisneros, Henry G. "The University and the Urban Challenge." *Cityscape: A Journal of Policy Development and Research*, Special Issue (December 1996): 1–14.

Citrin, Toby. "Enhancing Public Health Research and Learning Through Community-Academic Partnerships." *Public Health Reports* 116, no. 1 (2001): 74–78.

Collins, S., and M.P. Hornsby-Smith. "The Rise and Fall of the YCW in England." *Journal of Contemporary Religion* 19, no.1 (2002): 87–100.

Cox, David N. "Developing a Framework for Understanding University Community Partnerships." *Cityscape: A Journal of Policy Development and Research* 5, no. 1 (2000): 9–26.

Cox, David, and Melissa Pearce. "Promise with Caveats: Examining the Potential of Community-Higher Education Partnerships." Paper presented at the 2002 Annual Conference of the American Association of Colleges and Universities. Pittsburgh, PA. October 2002.

De Leon, Peter. *Advice and Consent: The Development of the Policy Sciences.* New York: Russel Sage, 1988.

Dewar, Margaret E., and Claudia B. Isaac. "The Potentially Transforming Experience of Community/University Collaboration." *Journal of Planning Education and Research* 17, no. 4 (1998): 334–47.

Driscoll, Amy, and Ernest Lynton. *Making Outreach Visible: A Guide to Documenting Professional Service and Outreach.* Washington, DC: American Association for Higher Education, 1999.

Farrish, Katherine. "Yale Takes a New Course, Investing in New Haven." *The Hartford Courant,* 30 August 1994.

Feld, Marcia Marker. "Community Outreach Partnership Centers: Forging New Relationships Between University and Community." *Journal of Planning Education and Research* 17, no. 4 (1998): 285–90.

Gamson, William. *The Strategy of Social Protest.* Belmont, CA: Wadsworth, 1990.

Gerlach, Luther, and Virginia Hine. *"Movements of Revolutionary Change: Some Structural Characteristics."* In *Social Movements of the Sixties and Seventies,* edited by J. Freeman, 133–45. New York: Longman, 1983.

Gladwell, Malcom. *The Tipping Point: How Little Things Can Make a Big Difference.* New York: Little Brown and Company, 2000.

Glassick, C. E., M. T. Humber, and G. I. Maeroff. *Scholarship Assessed: Evaluation of the Professoriate* (A Special Report of the Carnegie Foundation for the Advancement of Teaching). San Francisco: Jossey-Bass Publishers, 1997.

Goldsmith, Stephen. *The Twenty-First Century City: Resurrecting Urban America.* Lanham, MD: Roman and Littlefield, Inc, 1999.

Hackney, S. "The University and Its Community: Past and Present." *Annals of the American Academy* 488 (1986): 135–47.

Harkavy, Ira. "The Demands of the Times and the American Research University." *Journal of Planning Literature* 11, no. 3 (1997): 333–36.

———. "Dancing in the Shadows: The Integration of Academic Mission and Community Service." 1998a.

———. "Effectively Integrating Community Building and Education Reform." Joint Conference Connecting Community Building and University Partnership. 1998b.

Harkavy, Ira, and John L. Puckett. "Universities and the Inner Cities." *Planning for Higher Education* 20, no. 4 (1992): 27–32.

Hyland, Stanley, David Cox, and Cindy Martin. "Memphis Maps." *Metropolitan Universities Journal: An International Forum* 8, no. 4 (1998): 65–74.

Innes, Judith. "Planning Theory's Emerging Paradigm: Communicative Action and Interactive Practice." *Journal of Planning Education and Research* 14, no. 3 (1995): 183–89.

———. "Planning Through Consensus Building: A New View of the Comprehensive Planning Ideal." *Journal of the American Planning Association* 62, no. 4 (1996): 460–72.

Kolb, David. *Experiential Learning: Experience as the Source of Learning and Development.* Englewood Cliffs, NJ: Prentice-Hall, 1984.

Kretzmann, John P., and John L. McKnight. *Building Communities from the Inside Out: A Path Toward Finding and Mobilizing Community Assets.* Evanston, IL: Neighborhood Innovations Network, Center for Urban Affairs and Policy Research, Northwestern University, 1993.

Kupiec, T.Y., ed. *Rethinking Tradition: Integrating Service with Academic Study on College Campuses.* Providence, RI: Campus Compact, Education Commission of the States, 1993.

Lofland, John. *Social Movement Organizations.* New York: Aldine De Gruyter, 1996.

Lynton, Ernest A. *Making the Case for Professional Service.* Washington, DC: American Association for Higher Education, 1995.

Lynton, Ernest A., and Sandra E. Elman. *The New Priorities for the University.* San Francisco: Jossey-Bass Publishers, 1987.

Markus, Gregory, Jeffrey Howard, and David King. "Integrating Community Service and Classroom Instruction Enhances Learning: Results from an Experiment." *Educational Evaluation and Policy Analysis* 15, no. 4 (1993): 410–19.

Marwell, Gerald, and Pamela Oliver. "Collective Action Theory and Social Movements Research." *Research in Social Movements, Conflict and Change* 7 (1984): 1–27.

Maurrasse, David J. *Beyond the Campus: How Colleges and Universities Form Partnerships with Their Communities.* New York: Routledge, 2001.

———. "Higher Education-Community Partnerships: Assessing Progress in the Field." *Nonprofit and Voluntary Sector Quarterly* 31, no. 1 (2002): 131–39.

Mollenkopf, John. *The Contested City.* Princeton, NJ: Princeton University Press, 1983.

Petchey, R., J. Williams, B. Farnswork, and K. Starkey. "A Tale of Two (Low Prevalence) Cities: Social Movement Organizations and the Local Policy Response to HIV/AIDS." *Social Science and Medicine* 47, no. 9 (1998): 1197–1208.

Potapchuk, William R., and Carolina G. Polk. *Building the Collaborative Community.* Washington, DC: The National Institute for Dispute Resolution and the Center for Community Problem Solving, 1994.

Putnam, Robert. "The Prosperous Community: Social Capital and Community Life." *American Prospect* (spring 1993): 35–42.

Reardon, Kenneth. "Enhancing the Capacity of Community Organizations in East St. Louis." *Journal of Planning Education and Research* 17, no. 4 (1998): 323–33.

Rosaen, Cheryl, Pennie Foster-Fishman, and Frank Fear. *Metropolitan Universities* 12, no. 4 (2001): 10–29.

Rosaldo, R. *Culture and Truth: The Remaking of Social Analysis.* Boston: Beacon Press, 1993.

Rose, Richard. "Comparing Forms of Comparative Analysis." *Political Studies* 39, no. 3 (1991): 446–62.

———. *Lesson-Drawing in Public Policy: A Guide to Learning Across Time and Space.* Chatham: Chatham House Publishers, Inc., 1993.

Schon. D. "The New Scholarship Requires a New Epistemology." *Change* 27 (1995): 27–34.

Stokes, Donald E. *Pasteur's Quadrant.* Washington, DC: Brookings Institution, 1997.

Swanstrom, Todd. "Beyond Economism: Urban Political Economy and the Postmodern Challenge." *Journal of Urban Affairs* 15, no. 1 (1993): 55–78.

CONTRIBUTORS

Jonathan Cohen is a programme manager for AccountAbility, a London-based international, multistakeholder membership organization consisting of businesses, non-governmental organizations, and academics, whose mission is promoting accountability for sustainable development. He is an advisory board member of the Center for Innovation in Social Responsibility, as well as founding chair of the Socially Responsible Business Alliance of New York. He is the founding content manager of the news link of the United Nations Global Compact web site and has served as a member of the national NGO committees concerning the U.N. International Year of Volunteers in 2001, the Five-Year Review of the U.N. Beijing Women's Conference in 2000, the U.N. International Year of Older Persons in 1999, and the Universal Declaration of Human Rights 50th anniversary in 1998.

Tyshammie Cooper is director of Program and Community Development at Corinthian Housing Development Corporation in Newark, New Jersey, where she creates community computer and technology programs that teach participants computer applications, job training and development skills, and educational test preparation techniques. She has been working in community development for the last five years and has been responsible for grant writing.

David N. Cox holds the rank of Professor in the division of Public Administration and serves as assistant to the president and provost for partnerships at the University of Memphis. He is chairman of the board of the Association for Community–Higher Education Partnerships and is a member of the National Review Board for the Scholarship of Engagement. He served on loan from the university as director of the Office of University Partnerships for the U.S. Department of Housing and Urban Development in 1998–99. His research, outreach, and publications have centered on the effect of urban governance structures on the responsiveness, equity, and effectiveness of public policies and on strategies for interorganizational collaboration.

Frank Dixon is a managing director at Innovest Strategic Value Advisors. He worked as a management consultant, specializing in the energy and manufacturing sectors, where his work included consulting on cost-effectively improving corporate environmental performance.

Allan J. Formicola is Professor of Periodontics and former dean of the Columbia University School of Dental and Oral Surgery, a position that he held for twenty-three years. Dr. Formicola currently is vice dean for the Center for Community Health Partnerships, a new center in the Faculty of Health Sciences of Columbia University. He has served as president of the American Association of Dental Schools (AADS), as the vice president of the Commission on Dental Accreditation, and chaired Accreditation Site Visit Teams, as well as served as consultant and member of the Pew Foundation's Commission on the Future of the Health Professions and as a consultant to the Veterans Administration.

Carol Glazer is a program development and management consultant to foundations, universities, and nonprofit organizations working to improve conditions in inner-city communities in the United States. Her clients have included the Rockefeller, Robert Wood

Johnson, and Goldman Sachs foundations; Harvard University; the Community Reinvestment Fund; and the Center for Alternative Sentencing and Employment Services. She has consulted in substantive areas of housing, work force development, education, and youth development.

Sandra Harris is the Executive Director of the Northern Manhattan Community Voices Collaborative.

Perry Mehrling is Professor of Economics at Barnard College, Columbia University, where he teaches and researches in the fields of monetary economics, financial economics, and history of economics. His most recent book is *The Money Interest and the Public Interest* (1998). He is currently at work on *The Price of Risk: Fischer Black and the Revolution in Modern Finance.* His work on foundation payout emerges from a larger project on the financial problems of the welfare state including Social Security, education finance, and health finance.

Walid Michelen is the Chief Medical Officer and Vice-President for Community Health at New York Presbyterian Hospital.

Osagie Kingsley Obasogie is a fellow in the Graduate of Opportunity Program at University of California, Berkeley. As a legal consultant for the Drug Policy Alliance (DPA) the nation's leading harm-reduction advocacy group, he currently conducts sociological and legal research in various areas of drug policy reform to advise the DPA on appropriate courses of action and advocacy. He also served as the articles editor and the book review editor for the *National Black Law Journal.*

Aida Rodriguez is a Professor of Professional Practice and the chair of the Nonprofit Management Program at the Robert J. Milano School of Management and Urban Policy, New School University. Formerly deputy director of the Equal Opportunity Division of the Rockefeller Foundation, she now serves on the APPAM Policy Council and Program Committee; is on the Steering Committee of the Nonprofit Academic Centers Council (NACC); serves as one of a small core of fellows in the Kellogg Foundation's Liderazco en Filantropia en las Americas international program; and is an advisor to philanthropic initiatives in the United States and in Latin America—including the Funders' Collaborative for Strong Latino Communities. She also serves on various nonprofit boards including One Economy, Inc., Learning Leaders, Inc., and CCRP, Inc.

Heather Bent Tamir is a communications associate at PolicyLink, a national nonprofit research, communications, capacity building, and advocacy organization and helps to produce speeches, articles, and books that advance PolicyLink goals in areas such as equitable development, wealth building, and racial equity. She also assists in establishing and maintaining effective media relations.

Index